Dating of Vintage Dretsch Drums Based Upon Serial Numbers: Challenging the Legend, Lore, and Lies
Richard E Gier

Fourth Edition, Updated 2023

©2023 by Richard E. Gier

ISBN 978-1-888408-61-4

Rebeats Publications
P/O/ Box 6
Alma, Michigan 48801
www.rebeats.com

COPYRIGHT INFRINGEMENT NOTICE

The first edition of this book suffered frequent infringement. The preparation of this information involved thousands of hours of hard work. The author retains all rights, including the right to reproduce, distribute, display, and sell this work and to create derivative works based upon this work. You cannot scan or take a picture of an important table or graph and post it on an internet site; that violates the author's intellectual property rights. This is not excused by fair use exceptions to U.S. Trademark law. It also does not matter that you did not make any money from that act- what matters is the impact on potential sales of this publication. **Please honor the author's creative rights!**

Cover photo credits:
Badge: Richard E. Gier
Serial Number label: Bill Maley of classicvintagedrums.com

TABLE OF CONTENTS

I. REVIEW OF CURRENT PRACTICES AND LITERATURE.......................... 2

II. THE SERIAL NUMBER LOG.. 5

III. HISTORY OF SERIAL NUMBERS.. 6

IV. ANALYSIS OF CHANGING PHYSICAL CHARACTERISTICS................11

    A. Characteristics   11

        1. Serial Number   11
        2. Badge Style   14
        3. Label Style   18
        4. Model Number   23
        5. Model Number – Stamped, Handwritten or Blank   24
        6. Model Number – Color of Ink   25
        7. Lug Casing Attachment Screw Head Type – Round or Hexagonal   27
        8. Wrap/Finish   28
        9. Two Headed vs. Concert Tom   29
        10. Throwoff / Strainer Type for Snare Drums   30
        11. Drum Dimensions   32
        12. Set Configuration   32
        13. Chrome Snares – Center Decorative Knurled Markings   32

    B. Oddballs and Anomalies   33

V. DATES LINKED TO GRETSCH DRUMS....................................... 34

VI. GRETSCH SERIAL NUMBER / DATE GUIDES............................ 38

VII. SHERIDAN'S RULE REFINED.. 43

VIII. BADGE TIMELINE REFINED... 44

IX. CONCLUSION.. 44

Dating of Vintage Gretsch[1] Drums Based Upon Serial Numbers – Challenging the Legend, Lore and Lies

© Richard E. Gier 2011, 2023

This represents the fourth edition of this guide. It utilizes 17 years of data collection with twice the number of drums as the first edition. Since its first publication in 2011, this guide has become the standard for dating of vintage Gretsch drums with serial numbers. It is important to understand the history of dating of Gretsch drums to not only avoid falling into old ways, but to understand how and why so many people are confused about how to determine the manufacture date of their drums.

> "Vintage Gretsch 12" shell only EXCELLENT NO EXTRA HOLES Up for grabs a nice clean NO EXTRA HOLES Gretsch 60's 8 X 12 5 lugs tom shell … The drum has a a [sic] 3/8" diameter hole for a badge, not a tacked on round badge, which indicates the drum is from the mid to later 60's, not early 60's. The serial number is 5 digits (14665)."
> *From actual eBay ad – misidentifying 1970s shell by dismissing vent hole from Stop Sign badge and misapplying common tool used for Round Badge era drums.*

> "GRETSCH 16" FLOOR TOM Blue Sparkle JASPER shell 60s SSB . . . Up for bids is a very rare find, it is a 1960's Blue sparkle Stop sign badge Gretsch Be Bop floor tom tom . . . This is a very sought after drum, original orange paper tag early 60's JASPER shell, this has 45 degree edges, I believe."
> *From actual eBay ad - a very rare find indeed, since the particular drum [SN 122456] was not from the "early 60's" but more likely not made until about 1969 or 1970 (and probably does not have 45 degree edges either).*

This paper reviews historical practices, literature and internet forum-based recommendations for approximating the date of manufacture of vintage Gretsch drums,[2] provides analysis of information collected from thousands of vintage drums and presents serial numbers as a reliable dating tool for the vintage drum enthusiast.

---

[1] Gretsch is a registered trademark of Fred W. Gretsch Enterprises Ltd. Although the ownership of the Gretsch brand has changed over the years, this article considers those drums produced under the Gretsch name from the early 1960s through the early 1980s. The author is not associated with the owner or licensees of the mark. All trademarks referenced in this paper are the property of their respective owners.

[2] All websites cited in the notes were re-visited on March 3, 2023, but information cited may have changed or may no longer be available when the reader visits these sites.

I. REVIEW OF HISTORICAL PRACTICES AND LITERATURE

Most recognized Gretsch drum experts wrote that serial numbers are not very useful in determining the age or manufacture date of Gretsch drums.[3] This belief was perpetuated, in part, because prior to about 2007, Gretsch's standard response to "How old is my drum?" inquiries stated that Gretsch was "unable to provide detailed production years of individual drums based on serial numbers."[4] The hopeful were told by Gretsch to date drums by the changes in badge styles through the years but were provided an incomplete list of badges.[5] Without the use of serial numbers, the general approach was to look at physical characteristics like badges, hardware, wraps, throwoffs/strainers, screw head types and the presence or absence of interior sealer.[6] Comparisons were made to catalogs,[7] information from Chet Falzerano's book and John Sheridan's articles, and the recollections and opinions of experts and enthusiasts on drum websites and discussion forums[8] - all well-intentioned, but not all accurate. While much of the

---

[3] Steve Maxwell, post on www.vintagedrumforum.com, November 28, 2005 (hereinafter "Maxwell vdf post") ("In terms of dating a kit the serial numbers on the paper tags are irrelevant since they were not placed on the drums in any sort of numerical order. They just grabbed a tag and glued it on the inside of the drum. Remember, they weren't building "collector's items" back then. They were just building drums and the whole issue of doing things in strict serial number order just didn't exist. It was not important to the process of building drums."). Chet Falzerano, Gretsch Drums, The Legacy of 'That Great Gretsch Sound, Centerstream Publishing, Fullerton, CA (1995), at page 55 (hereinafter "Falzerano") ("Identification by this number is impossible as no records remain at the Gretsch factory."); John Sheridan, "Badges??? We Don't Need No Stinkin' Badges" Classic Drummer (2007) (hereinafter "Badges Article") ("Unlike Gretsch's equally-famous guitar line, the drum serial numbers offer little clue to the actual dates of manufacture."); and John Sheridan, "Solving the Mystery of That Great Gretsch Sound," Not So Modern Drummer, (Fall 2005), pages 4-7 at 6 ("(T)hose serial numbers are next to useless in dating Gretsch drums.").

[4] The response states: "With two major fires at the Gretsch factories in the past, most of the historical records were destroyed including any documents referencing serial number details for drum production. Since these records are no longer available, we are unable to provide detailed production years of individual drums based on serial numbers." Reprinted at http://www.vintagedrumguide.com/gretsch_badges_timeline.html. Note that the fires reportedly occurred in 1972 and 1973 according to one source (Richard Egart, "Inside Gretsch - A Visit to the Gretsch Factory," Modern Drummer Magazine, May 1984, p 18, reprinted at http://www.gretschdrums.com/ebooks/1984/index.html (the "Centennial Article")) and January and December 1973 according to another (John Sheridan, email exchange November 19, 2010).

[5] Gretsch still provides a badge timeline which largely mirrors that provided in the Centennial Article. http:/www.gretschdrums.com/history.

[6] http://www.vintagedrumguide.com/serial_numbers.html (suggests dating based upon physical characteristics rather than serial numbers).

[7] Catalogs with copyright/issuance dates 1963 (#42), 1966 (#43), 1969 (#44), 1971 (#45), 1971 (Supplement), 1977, 1981, and later exist. There is some disagreement regarding the actual issue dates and uncertainty regarding how up-to-date the information in drum catalogs was at the time of publication. For example, Gretsch issued pricelists in 1968 and 1980 which expressly referred to the catalogs which are general considered to be from 1969 and 1981, respectively. The 1971 catalog contains a 1971 date in the copyright notice, which should indicate the date of first publication of the catalog, but many of the catalogs lack copyright notices. There may also be some time gap between the taking and gathering of pictures and the publication of the catalog. Images of some Gretsch catalogs are available at: http://www.gretschdrums.com/history.html, http://www.vintagedrumguide.com/gretsch_drumsets.html and at http://www.drumarchive.com/Gretsch/.

[8] i.e.: www.drumforum.org, www.vintagedrumforum.com.

information available was helpful, some of it was also contradictory, and little of it was definitive. Opinions were often strongly expressed, even when not supported by hard facts. Gaps in facts were filled by fuzzy memories, speculation and guesses, which eventually became part of the legend and lore of vintage Gretsch drums.

Despite the general discounting of the usefulness of serial numbers and his own comments to the contrary, at least one person suggested serial numbers could be reliably used to estimate manufacture dates. John Sheridan's rule of thumb for Round Badge drums – "four or less digits = early-'60s; five digits = mid-'60s, and six digits = late-'60s" ("Sheridan's Rule") - was the most accepted guide.[9] In 2011 Gretsch's website featured Sheridan's Badges Article, so Gretsch apparently approved of the Sheridan's Rule methodology.[10] Sheridan's Rule's scope is limited to the 1960s time period, which avoids some of the confusion introduced by Gretsch's later reuse of serial numbers.[11] In his Badges Article, Sheridan also provides a very useful timeline of Gretsch's progression through different badge styles from the 1930s through 2007. Sheridan's work is a step up from Gretsch's prior "official" information and the Centennial Article. It also expanded and refined the badge timeline provided by David Anfuso at www.vintagedrumguide.com.[12] However, while Sheridan linked dates to badge styles and provided a useful tool for one decade of drums, Round Badge drum owners armed with only Sheridan's Rule were left with at best a broad range of possible years of manufacture. Owners of later drums continued to disregard the serial numbers or speculate about what their numbers represent.

This situation was particularly frustrating because information was available for other major US manufacturers. Rob Cook and others addressed Ludwig drums.[13] Dr. Carl J. Wenk analyzed Slingerland serial numbers and provided a very useful framework.[14] A similar effort existed for Rogers.[15] However, even where strong correlations have been established between serial numbers and dates, these tools do not provide foolproof or exact dates. All manufacturers have their unexplained exceptions. Reportedly, Ludwig and Slingerland badges were simply grabbed out of bins and not

---

[9] Badges Article.
[10] www.gretschdrums.com/history. The Gretsch site no longer cites Sheridan's Rule.
[11] Gretsch used some of the same serial numbers three times during the period from the late 1960s to the 1980s.
[12] http://www.vintagedrumsguide.com/gretsch_badges.html.
[13] Rob Cook, The Ludwig Book, Rebeats Publications, Alma, MI (2003), page 210. Serial Number chart reprinted (with errors and no credit to Mr. Cook) at https://www.ludwig-drums.com/en-us/ludwig-serial-guide; Ned Ingberman, "How to Date 1960's Ludwig Drums by Serial Numbers." DRUM Magazine, September/October 2002, reprinted at www.vintagedrum.com/ludwig_serials/. Both serial numbers date charts and a third from the defunct site www.LudwigDrummer.com are at http://vintagedrumguide.com/serial_numbers.html. The author added another resource – Richard E. Gier, Serial Number Based Dating Guides for Vintage Ludwig Drums, Main Line Drums 1963-1984 & Standard Drums 1968-1973, Rebeats Publications, Alma, Michigan, 2013.
[14] Carl Wenk, "Slingerland Serial Numbers," https://www.vintagedrumguide.com/drcjw/article_2_serial_numbers_page1.html.
[15] See thread on the Rogers Owners Forum http://www.runboard.com/brogersownersforum.t3597.

used in numerical order.[16] Misplaced boxes of Ludwig badges were reportedly used years later, making them appear "out of order."[17] Drums or shells may have sat in factory inventory or drum shops only to be matched up with newer drums in order to make a sale or fill a customer's request. Ludwig in particular has a reputation for not letting anything go to waste, leading to configurations and combinations that stand apart from the norm.[18] Everyone involved with vintage drums has heard the explanations and should understand that determining a drum's manufacture date using its serial number is at best an approximation. Yet, we still desire more precision and accuracy.

Despite all of the attention to the other manufacturers, there had been no comprehensive dating guide developed for Gretsch drums. It appears that after encountering 1970s Stop Sign badge drums or 1980s Square Badge drums with lower serial numbers than 1960s Round Badge drums, many vintage drum experts simply threw out the serial numbers as an unexplainable and unhelpful bit of vintage drum trivia.[19] It is difficult to understand why this happened when Ludwig, Rogers and Slingerland's reuse of serial numbers is well documented and generally accepted.[20] It appears that no one understood how Gretsch reused serial numbers. Strangely, while disregarding the usefulness of serial numbers, many in the vintage drum community embraced Sheridan's Rule, which is premised upon serial numbers having meaning.

The lack of clear understanding led to an environment with an amazing amount of conflicting (and often incorrect) information. Some who sold vintage Gretsch drums filled the void by declaring with apparent precision the year of manufacture of their offerings.[21] Some date claims seemed intentionally fraudulent, since 1960's Round Badge drums sell for a significant premium over their 1970's Stop Sign Badge brethren. One eBay seller routinely described the majority of the Stop Sign Badge drums they offered as being made in the late1960s/early1970s, even though most were clearly not made in the 1960s. Further, claims were so frequent that a Stop Sign badge drum was "among the first made" with that badge and therefore possessed the Round Badge mystique, that one might conclude Gretsch produced thousands of drums every day in the early 1970s and then sat idle for the much of the rest of the decade. Other date claims were likely just a result of reliance upon the vast amount of incorrect information which pervaded the internet on this subject or the misapplication of the few tools that were available. Still other sellers appeared to be just making stuff up because there was no one who could contradict them. When questioned about their age representations, sellers cited

---

[16] Cook and Ingberman, note 13 (Ludwig), Wenk, note 14 and Wenk, http://www.vintagedrumguide.com/drcjw/article_1_text.html (Slingerland).

[17] Ingberman, note 13.

[18] John Aldridge, Guide to Vintage Drums, Centerstream Publishing, Fullerton, CA (1994) page 70.

[19] It is interesting to note that both Cook and Wenk acknowledge that the common belief at the time they began their data collection was that serial numbers on Ludwig and Slingerland, respectively, had no meaning.

[20] http://www.vintagedrumguide.com/drcjw/article_2_serial_numbers_page1.html (Slingerland); Cook, note 13 and http://www.vintagedrumguide.com/ludwig_standards.htm (Ludwig - new sequence of numbers used for Standard line and periods with no serial numbers on early Blue/Olive badges); and serial number chart cited in note 15 (Rogers).

[21] One particular dealer routinely states a precise year of manufacture for their Round Badge Gretsch offerings, but does not offer supporting information or respond to questions about their date claims.

Sheridan's Rule, explained that they talked to their "local vintage drum expert," claimed personal knowledge based upon years of experience dealing drums, admitted that they are just guessing, or failed to respond at all. A rare few could produce original dated receipts or reliable histories for their drums or provide any sort of justification for their date claims.

> **Dating of Gretsch drums was uneven at best. Some were just trying to do their best with the inadequate information available. Many just made stuff up, either to make their drums appear more valuable or to make themselves appear more intelligent.**

It was into this morass that the author stumbled when he picked up a dirty Gretsch drum set at an auction.[22] He joined the frustrated ranks of Gretsch drum owners who wanted to know something definitive about their drums and decided to attempt to fill the void.[23]

II. THE SERIAL NUMBER LOG

In late 2006, the author started compiling a modest database of Gretsch Round Badge drums. A search for others who might be able to shed some light on the subject was conducted. An existing thread on the topic was located on the drum-related website www.drumforum.org ("DFO"). Earlier that year, forum member Greg Webb started a log of serial numbers and other characteristics of Round Badge era drums, asking forum members for information about their drums.[24] The author contacted Webb and efforts were combined. The author took the lead of the data gathering and cataloging function, with Webb providing support and review. Over time, the information collected grew to include thirteen specific items, though not all information was available for all drums. Notes recorded additional information which was available.

As of this fourth edition, the main log contains more than 8,600 drums which appear to be unaltered or have histories which are clearly explained. Of these, more than 4,200 have or originally had Round Badges. This represents over 3.6% of the approximately 116,000 Round Badge drums which have serial numbers. The inclusion of Stop Sign Badge and Square Badge drums in the log helped to support the analysis of the Round Badge era drums and expand the coverage of the guide.

Entries for just over 180 drums are segregated from the main log. Some serial numbers are difficult to read or missing critical digits due to damaged labels. Other drums are reportedly rewrapped or rebadged, or appear significantly altered in other ways. Some drums have so little information or lack so many parts, whether badges,

---

[22] An original RB 12/14/20 Progressive Jazz set in Silver Glass Glitter purchased for $12.50.
[23] The author readily acknowledges that he does not possess knowledge based upon decades of dealing vintage drums or playing those same drums before they were "vintage." The author has great respect for those who have that knowledge. However, this paper offers a fresh perspective that strives to be relatively free from the legend and lore of vintage drums.
[24] The original DFO thread regarding the Serial Number Log is no longer available.

hardware, wraps or even shells,[25] that it was difficult to utilize the information. Reproduction badges and labels further confuse the issue.[26] Some owners are open about the counterfeit or replacement labels and badges on their drums,[27] but many are likely purposefully silent or simply unaware that their drums are altered. Some drums are not included in the main log because the information and descriptions are considered unreliable. Some sellers simply make things up. A select few eBay sellers have earned unfavorable reputations by repeatedly offering drums with undisclosed modifications, so all of their listings are flagged.[28] All of the segregated drums are repeatedly reviewed to determine if they are anomalies or merely contain incorrect information. Since vintage drums are not always known to fit neatly contrived, orderly explanations, it would be a mistake to simply ignore the drums which do not fit the neat patterns. A serious effort is made to include these drums in the main log, even if they complicate or contradict the overall analysis. The information on some drums, after repeated review, is deemed too unreliable to be included.

After five years of collecting and analyzing the information, it is clear why confusion ruled. However, a great deal of order could be brought to the chaos. The original guide provided a reliable tool for estimating a drum's age for later Round Badge era, Stop Sign Badge era, and early Square Badge era drums. This revised guide uses twice as many reports of vintage drums gathered over an additional twelve years to support its observations. No attempt is made here to create a comprehensive history of all things Gretsch. The serial number-based dating methodology presented in this guide is included in The Gretsch Drum Book, the most complete resource on the subject.[29] No claim is made to the absolute and complete accuracy of every bit of information included here. Even the sources cited herein, which are widely accepted as the most reliable on the subject, contain contradictions. Where assumptions and guesses are made by the author, an attempt is made to identify them as such.

III. HISTORY OF SERIAL NUMBERS

A. The Start of Serial Numbers and Labels. Different drum companies addressed serialization in different ways and started it at different times. Rogers and

---

[25] Labels removed from Gretsch drums are readily available. Reproduction labels are made by some drum owners with scanners, printers and a little computer know-how. Note that these reproductions are likely not authorized and may represent violations of trademark rights of the owners of the marks.

[26] While original badges are actively bought and sold, reproduction badges are also available. Like reproduction labels, the reproduction badges likely violate rights of the holders of the Gretsch trademarks.

[27] One seller openly disclosed that he had crafted Gretsch copies using Keller shells and vintage hardware, complete with counterfeit labels, using his birthdate (51155) as the serial number on all three drums in the set. Another seller recently offered a rewrapped 12/14/18 set with "reproduction labels" with "correct" serial numbers and model numbers [whatever that means – a question seeking clarification was ignored]. It seems that reproduction labels are often attached to drums that are unoriginal in multiple other ways, including undisclosed floor tom conversions to 14x18 bass drums.

[28] One seller has a reputation for rewrapping shells in new wrap and advertising them as "original," rationalizing that the wrap is made by the same company which supplied Gretsch decades before. Badges are often switched as well on his offerings. All of this seller's drums have been segregated from the main log.

[29] Rob Cook with John Sheridan, The Gretsch Drum Book, Rebeats Press, 2013.

Gretsch printed serial numbers on paper labels which were glued to the inside of shells while Ludwig and Slingerland stamped serial numbers into the badges which were affixed to the outside of their drums. It has been reported that in the early 1960s, insurance companies, school customers or governmental regulation urged drum manufacturers to apply serial numbers as unique identifiers for their drums,[30] but no strong evidence has surfaced for exactly why drum companies began to use serial numbers.[31] Rogers' use of serial numbers pre-dates any 1960's mandate, as Rogers applied labels with serial numbers when in production in Covington, OH as early as 1953.[32] Slingerland followed in 1962 and Ludwig joined in by late 1963 or early 1964.[33] Gretsch serial numbers first appeared around 1962, possibly earlier.[34]

For purposes of this guide, 1962 is utilized as the start date. Reliable date reports of labeled drums may shift this date. It is possible that labels were introduced earlier and that lower production rates in the late 1950s and early 1960s, before The Beatles' appearance on Ed Sullivan in 1964 increased demand for drums, would support moving the date of the initial appearance of serial numbers and labels earlier than 1962.

In addition to basing this date upon the dating information developed later in this paper, analysis of some significant changes of the 1950s provides further support for an early 1960s start date of Gretsch's labels. Although there is no precise timeline indicating when the use of interior silver sealer paint commenced or when changes in the shell construction from 3-ply to 6-ply occurred, we can determine the order in which they occurred. Maxwell places all three changes in 1957-58.[35] Falzerano places all three changes in the mid-1950s but is not very specific about when each occurred.[36] Sheridan estimates that the ply change occurs in about 1959[37] and labels started in 1961-62.

Reconciling these experts' opinions and other anecdotal evidence to produce refined date estimates requires some subjective reasoning. Date stamps on the interior of

---

[30] See Ingberman, note 13, http://www.vintagedrumguide.com/serial_numbers.html.
[31] Richard E. Gier, "Were American Drum Manufacturers Required by Law to Use Serial Numbers During the 1960s?" June 16, 2020. available at https://www.gretschdrumdatingguide.com/other-projects.html and https://www.notsomoderndrummer.com/not-so-modern-drummer/2020/6/16/were-american-drum-manufacturersnbsprequired-by-law-to-use-serial-numbers-during-the-1960s.
[32] Serial numbers were instituted after Grossman Music Corp. (Henry Grossman/Cleveland, OH) purchased the Rogers trade name and machinery from Joseph Rogers Jr. & Son (Cleveland S. Rogers/Farmingdale, NJ) upon the passing of the owner in 1952. Mr. Grossman named his company Joseph Rogers, Inc. and advertised serial numbers inside as a selling point for his drums. Per Gary Nelson, drum historian, this was found in a late 1952 eight-page mailer/advertisement for 1953. Email exchanges with Gary Nelson, September 17, 2009 – February 22, 2011.
[33] See sources cited in notes 13 and 14 above.
[34] The earliest verifiable report of Gretsch serial numbers is a receipt dated November 1962 for drums with serial numbers in the 4200 or 4400 range. David Anfuso wrote: "There has been a lot of discussion about this and some contradicting information. But the general consensus [sic] is that the paper tags started sometime around 1962 or 1963." http://vintagedrumguide.com/painting_shell_interiors.html. Sheridan's Rule provides an "early 1960s" date for the introduction of labels and John Sheridan estimates that labels began in 1961-62. Email correspondence with John Sheridan, July 29, 2011.
[35] Maxwell vdf post.
[36] Falzerano, p. 53-54 (quoting Phil Grant and Bill Hagner, Gretsch employees).
[37] Email correspondence with John Sheridan, July 29, 2011.

unpainted shells had been standard up until late 1953, with few if any shells having later date stamps. The author owned a 3-ply Cocktail drum with silver sealer known to be made no later than 1955.[38] The author suggests that early 1954 is a reasonable estimate for the beginning of the use of silver sealer.

Unlabeled 3-ply and 6-ply shells with the silver sealer exist, but precisely how many of each were made is hard to gauge because without serial numbers, it is difficult to distinguish between individual drums of the same model and finish. The switch in number of plies was not sudden, and apparently involved experimentation with 4- and 5-ply shells as well.[39] Sheridan documents a 3-ply Cadillac Green set from September 1958, so at least some 3-ply shells were still in use at that time. Therefore, it is estimated the change in shell construction to 6-plies occurred sometime around 1958. So, by about 1958, Gretsch is producing drums with 6-ply shells with interior silver sealer but no labels. Based upon significant numbers of drums that fit this description, labels are not added for a few years, bringing us to about 1962.

Therefore, it appears that Gretsch began painting the shell interiors with silver sealer in about 1954. Next, shell construction changes from 3-ply to 6-ply in about 1958. Finally, labels are applied starting in about 1962.

B. The Application of Serial Numbers. The reported practice of haphazardly dumping badges into bins by Ludwig and Slingerland that results in so much date uncertainty seems to have been imputed onto Gretsch. Precisely why what other companies were doing with their metal badges should impact what Gretsch was doing with its paper labels is puzzling. Metal badges were in use by all major manufacturers for decades before serial numbers were initiated. It seems reasonable to assume that all of the major drum manufacturers' production lines were set up long before serial numbers came into use. The practice of dumping fresh badges into bins would not impact the finished drum – each one received a badge, and all involved were content. Only when badges began to have serial numbers on them would this process make any difference. When Ludwig and Slingerland began putting serial numbers on their badges, it appears that they did not drastically alter their procedures to control the sequential use of serial numbered badges. They reportedly continued to dump badges into bins and pull them out randomly, resulting in numerical and timing variations which frustrate vintage drum collectors today.

> **What Ludwig and Slingerland did with their serialized badges had no impact on what Gretsch did with their serialized paper labels.**

Unburdened with serial numbers on their badges, Gretsch and Rogers could continue to apply badges without a concern about getting them "out of order." However, since their serial numbers were on paper labels, a new step would be added to their production processes. In the 1960s, a logical place for Gretsch's label application is after the interior sealer is applied and after the determination of a shell's size and style is

---

[38] A picture showing the drum in use and dated 1955 accompanied the drum when it was purchased.
[39] Falzerano, p. 53.

made.[40] One can only speculate precisely where in the process labels were applied during the 1960s.[41] The few sources that might provide some insight into this question are silent on the subject. Gretsch's 1966 catalog (#43) fails to show the label application step among its several pictures of the drum making process in Brooklyn. An extensive description of a tour of the Gretsch plant in 1984 makes no mention of the application of the label, but places the application of the silver interior sealer late in the process.[42] Very few incorrect model numbers have been reported and recorded in the log, so it seems very likely the labels were applied after all other determinations were made.[43]

Gretsch labels were likely ordered from a label supplier pre-printed with serial numbers. Many of the labels show perforated top and bottom edges, which make sense for strip or roll stock. There are many reasons to believe that the labels were ordered and printed in numerical order. Despite changes to the labels themselves, the numerical sequence of serial numbers remained intact. There is no duplication of numbers at transition points between label styles. There was no need to restart serial numbers simply because the label style changed. The label printer was likely told the highest number from the prior order so that the next group of labels would not duplicate numbers which had already been used. Finally, with two notable exceptions discussed below, there are not large blocks of serial numbers missing from the log.

C. Were Gretsch Serial Numbers Used in Numerical Order? While the legend and lore of vintage drums cast heavy doubt on the usefulness of Gretsch serial numbers, the drums themselves tell a different story. Many indicators suggest that Gretsch used serial numbers in roughly numerical order, even if not in strict numerical order. Even though there is logical support for an orderly progression of serial numbers in their purchasing and printing, there is no specific reason to project that into a belief that the labels were then applied to drums in numerical order. It appears that rolls of labels were issued to the individual(s) responsible for applying them to the drums. If more than one person or work station was responsible for applying labels, multiple rolls would have been active at any given time. The manufacturing process appears to have been a make-to-inventory system, with the fixtures set to make many of the same size drum to fill inventory before switching the machinery fixtures or jigs to produce another size of drum.[44] This was long before Just-In-Time manufacturing principles became

---

[40] Since not all drum shells of a particular size had the same hardware or finish options, the model number determination might not have been made until long after the shell was cut to its final dimensions. For example, a 14x20 bass drum shell could become a model number 4249 separate tension / separate lug, a model number 4267 center guide / single tension Playboy model, or a model number 4255 center lug, separate tension Renown model bass drum.

[41] In the 1970s, model numbers were no longer stamped but handwritten on the labels. Therefore, it is possible the labels were applied earlier in the process, before a final determination of model number was made. This approach seems unlikely because the operator would have been required to reach inside the drum to complete the label. In the later Square Badge era when a finish code became a part of the model number, the label would most likely have been applied late in the production process.

[42] See Centennial Article.

[43] Only thirty of over 8,600 recorded drums appear to have been assigned incorrect model numbers. Most of these appear in the later portion of the log.

[44] For RB drums, when consecutive numbers appeared in the log, the model numbers and sizes tended to be the same. One hundred and forty of the 169 (83%) recorded pairs of round badge drums with consecutive

commonplace in the US.⁴⁵ Drums were then pulled from inventory to make sets to fill orders. This would result in many sets that had serial numbers which were relatively, but not extremely, close together.

The author has no illusion that the serial numbers were religiously applied in precise numerical order, but suggests it is human nature and good manufacturing procedure to want to use the serial numbers in order. If the labels were in fact supplied as strip or roll stock, then the worker would be all but forced to apply them in numerical order, at least within blocks of numbers, i.e.: someone grabbing a roll of 1,000 labels with serial numbers 50001 – 51000 likely used them in numerical order. When that roll was consumed, the next roll in order would likely have been selected.

It is interesting to note that in the same Brooklyn building, and later in the same Arkansas complex, Gretsch was making guitars and banjos along with its drums. Edward Ball, Gretsch guitar researcher, has documented that serial numbers were strictly controlled for guitars and banjos.⁴⁶ Models were generally produced in batches of 100. The serial numbers were assigned and logged to specific batches and completed labels were issued to the production floor. Unfortunately, it is difficult to determine how similar the processes for issuing serial numbers were for drums and guitars/banjos.

Even if the serial numbers were ordered in numerical order and applied in roughly numerical order as batches of drums were made, it is highly unlikely that drums were then shipped from inventory in any sort of strict serial number order. Orders would have generally been filled from inventory, likely with little to no regard for the serial numbers inside. The Centennial Article states that the process in place in 1983 included serial numbers on control tags which were used for tracking of drums from finished goods through shipment to the customer. However, there is no indication that serial numbers were considered when determining which drum to ship. The link between serial number and date would be diminished depending upon the amount of time particular sizes and finishes of drums sat in the warehouse before they were shipped to dealers and then sat for more time at dealers before finally being sold. The variation of time spent in inventory has significant potential to further diminish the link between manufacture date, serial number and date of sale at retail to the ultimate customer.

---

serial numbers had the same model number. In later years, the vast majority of drums with consecutive serial numbers were different model numbers, often described as coming together in factory issued sets. Although these observations can be at most characterized as tendencies, they suggest that in the 1960s someone might be making a particular model of drum and applying consecutive numbers to them. Once enough of that model had been completed, the fixtures would be changed and that person might start making a different model and pick up where they left off with the next label. During the later 1970s and 1980s, a single person may have been responsible for building all of the drums for a particular set configuration, and therefore may have produced more closely numbered sets as a result or the labels were prepared with the finished set in mind. Lower production volume may have also contributed to tighter groups of serial numbers in later years. These are just theories, but offer possible explanations for the observed tendencies.

⁴⁵ This is consistent with the phenomenon noted with consecutive serial numbers described in the prior note and the catalog pictures showing many work-in-process shells of the same size and finish drums stacked together partially through the manufacturing process.

⁴⁶ Edward Ball, Gretsch 6120 The History of a Legendary Guitar, Schiffer Books, 2010.

While it appears that serial numbers were used in the manufacturing process in roughly sequential order, one must acknowledge that drums were not likely sold in strict serial number order. Nonetheless, it is suggested that the link between serial number and date is meaningful and should not be disregarded.

IV. ANALYSIS OF CHANGING PHYSICAL CHARACTERISTICS

A. Characteristics.

To fully understand Gretsch's use of serial numbers, one must understand the other changes which took place over time with Gretsch drums. Many different characteristics changed as Gretsch moved through the 1960s and 1970s and into the 1980s. Ten different specific characteristics were tracked for all drums while others were noted when applicable. The characteristics are:

1. Serial Number
2. Badge Style
3. Label Style
4. Model Number
5. Model Number – Stamped, Handwritten or Blank
6. Model Number – Color of Ink
7. Lug Casing Attachment Screw Head Type – Round or Hexagonal
8. Wrap/Finish
9. Two Headed vs. Concert Tom
10. Throwoff / Strainer Type for Snare Drums
11. Drum Dimensions
12. Set Configuration
13. Chrome Snares – Center Decorative Knurled Markings.

Changes which occurred with each characteristic are isolated and analyzed below. The analysis starts with serial numbers and builds upon that foundation. Tables which link various characteristics are presented throughout and then all characteristics are combined into one master log. This master log presents the progression of several of the characteristics.

1. Serial Number.

Gretsch reused serial numbers, with most serial numbers appearing three times from the early 1960s through the 1980s. Restarts occurred in about 1971 and about 1984. It is apparent that Gretsch used serial numbers in roughly numerical order each time it worked through the sequences. When Gretsch changed a physical characteristic like label style, badge style, wrap/finish or type of hardware, those changes are closely linked to particular serial number ranges. With remarkably few exceptions, there are clear and distinct serial numbers which represent the transition points for these changing characteristics. If serial numbers were not issued sequentially, these distinct serial number transition points would not be identifiable. Likewise, original receipts and reports of original purchase dates of drums with known serial numbers track consistently with time. The later the drum sold, the later the serial number is in the orderly sequence. It is important to emphasize that the higher serial numbers are not necessarily indicative of later drums. The use and reuse of serial numbers must be understood to place drums in their proper order.

    a.   <u>The First Serial Number Sequence</u>. The first sequence of serial numbers (the "First Sequence") began with the introduction of labels, which is believed to have occurred in about 1962. During the First Sequence, the numbers started at about 1001[47] and continued uninterrupted through about 136500. The First Sequence lasted about ten years, from about 1961/62 until about 1971, with the initial eight years involving Round Badge (RB) drums and the remaining years involving the first style of Stop Sign Badge (SSB#1). It is during this First Sequence that Sheridan's Rule applies for Round Badge drums - four digit serial numbers are early 60s, five digit are mid-60s and six digit are late 60s.

    b.   <u>The Second Serial Number Sequence</u>. The second serial number sequence (the "Second Sequence") started at around 00001[48] and continued through about 148500, with the block between 92000 and 98000 absent from the log. The Second Sequence spanned over a decade, from about 1971 through about 1984, and involved three styles of Stop Sign Badges and two styles of Square Badges.

    c.   <u>The Third Serial Number Sequence</u>. The third time through serial numbers (the "Third Sequence") was a bit different than the first two. The Third Sequence started with about number 19780.[49] The block of serial numbers from 1 to 19779 is conspicuously absent from the log of more than 8,600 drums. No solid explanation exists for the jump, but ample opportunities exist for speculation. It is possible that several rolls of labels were lost or this block of numbers was skipped in the label ordering process. It is also possible that these numbers were not captured in a log originally designed for Round Badge drums and later expanded adapted to include other badge styles. No matter the reason, about 20,000 numbers are missing. Once started, the Third Sequence of serial numbers progressed in numerical order, although the end of the Third Sequence was not captured in this study. It is estimated that the Third Sequence began in about 1984.

    d.   <u>Later Serial Numbers</u>. From what can be observed with recent Gretsch serial numbers, new schemes were introduced, sometimes with the production year used as part of the serial number. This system sure makes it much easier and would have been handy had it appeared in the 1960s. It will be left to Gretsch or a modern drum enthusiast to report on these.

---

[47] The lowest reported serial number in this sequence is 01019. While there are 56 drums between 1000 and 2000, none have been reported between 0 and 1000. Therefore, the numbers are started at 1001.
[48] The lowest Second Sequence serial number recorded is 00015.
[49] In the Third Sequence, 19780, 19815, 19839, 19857, 19869, 19874 and 19984 are the only reported serial numbers below 20000. Others very likely exist.

e. <u>Leading Zeros</u>. At times during the early phases of both the First and Second Sequences Gretsch placed zeros in front of the meaningful digits of the serial number. The initial serial numbers of the First Sequence, from about 1000 to about 7000,[50] appeared as four digit numbers without leading zeros. At around number 7000,[51] a leading zero was added, making the serial number appear as a five digit number with a zero as the first digit, i.e.: serial number 9230 became serial number 09230. During the Second Sequence, enough leading zeros were added to make all serial numbers under 10000 five digits long,[52] i.e.: serial number 54 would become 00054 and 706 would become 00706. We do not know if Gretsch did this again in the Third Sequence, as that range of serial numbers is absent from the log.

Figures 1 and 2. Labels with First Sequence Serial Numbers
Without Leading Zero   With Leading Zero
(photo by author)   (photo by Bill Maley)

Figure 3. Label with Second Sequence Serial Number with One Leading Zero
(photo by Bill Maley)

The presence or absence of leading zeros provides a helpful dating tip. The absence of leading zeros on a serial number less than 10000 indicates a drum from the First Sequence. The presence of leading zeros on a serial number less than number 7000 indicates a drum from the Second Sequence. Unfortunately, the leading zeros on serial

---

[50] None of the 263 drums recorded from 1019 through 6990 in the First Sequence have leading zeros. There is a small amount of overlap - Serial number 07037 has a leading zero, but 7050 lacks a leading zero.
[51] All 98 drums recorded from 07058 through 09967 in the First Sequence have leading zeros.
[52] All 261 drums recorded from 00015 through 09979 in the Second Sequence have leading zeros.

numbers from about 7000 to 9999 appear the same whether from the First or Second Sequence.

Other than the way in which leading zeros appeared from 00001 to 07000, the labels used during the early part of the Second Sequence, from 07000 through about 51100, are indistinguishable from those of the First Sequence. They used the same style of paper label. Therefore, from about serial number 7000 through about 51100, one must look to other characteristics to determine is a drum is from the First or Second Sequence.

f. <u>Why Were Serial Numbers Reset?</u> Since few understood the reuse of serial numbers by Gretsch, fewer still have speculated why serial numbers were reset. There was no obvious reason to restart them, as six digits were already in use, one could continue up to 999999 before needing more room for another digit. The author once offered a theory on an internet forum that Gretsch's labels may have fallen victim to one of the 1973 plant fires so, to avoid the risk of short term duplication of numbers, and not recognizing the havoc it would later play when the drums reached vintage status, someone decided to start over at 1. It seemed like a logical connection and the timing seemed about right. The problem with expressing this theory was that someone believed it to be fact. The author found that he was unintentionally adding to the legend and the lore of Gretsch serial numbers. Gretsch may have just switched label suppliers who started the number sequences over. No definitive explanation has been uncovered to explain the reason that serial numbers were reset or reset again a decade later.

Understanding the reuse of serial numbers by Gretsch and appreciation for the ranges of each of the Serial Number Sequences provides insight into the overall system and begins to bring some order to the chaos.

Table 1
Serial Number Sequences
© Richard E. Gier 2011, 2023

Serial Number Sequence	Approximate Serial Number Range
First Sequence	1001 - 136500
Second Sequence	00001 - 148500*
Third Sequence	~19780 - higher

* No reported serial numbers between 92000 and 98000 in the Second Sequence.

2. Badge Style.

Gretsch used multiple different styles of badges to identify and brand their drums. Gretsch badges are the primary identifier used to distinguish between different eras of drums. Much is already known about Gretsch's use of badges. Egart provided a timeline in his 1984 Centennial Article. This same information was provided by Gretsch in email responses to those who asked about dating their drums. In 2007, Sheridan's Badges Article outlined in detail the progression of badge styles from Round Badge [1930-1970] ("RB"), Stop Sign Badge #1 [1971-1978] ("SSB#1"), Stop Sign Badge #2 [1978-79] ("SSB#2"), Square Badge #1 [1979] ("SQB#1"), Stop Sign Badge #3 – the Drop G

[1979] ("SSB#3"), and the Square badge resuming in the 1980s ("SQB#2").[53] With one exception - the SQB#1 badge preceded rather than followed the SSB#2 badge - and some shifting of the dates, the badge timelines presented by Egart and Sheridan seem to be reasonably precise.[54] Although other versions of the Gretsch badge exist before and after those shown here,[55] the badges listed above cover the entire time period addressed in this paper. At this point, only the comparison to serial numbers is presented. Later, once a timeline is developed, a revised badge timeline is presented along with a comparison to the timelines from the Centennial Article, the Badges Article and the one formerly provided by Gretsch.[56]

Figure 4. Round Badge
(photo by author)

Figure 5. Stop Sign Badge #1
(photo by Steve Traversi)

Figure 6. Square Badge #1
(photo by Rob Cook)

Figure 7. Stop Sign Badge #2
(photo by Adam Willis)

---

[53] This paper adopts most of the same abbreviations for badge and label styles presented by Sheridan. Sheridan's timeline represents an improvement over information formerly provided by Gretsch and the badge timeline currently available at http://www.vintagedrumguide.com/gretsch_badges.html. It generally agrees with the badge timeline presented by Egart in his Centennial Article.
[54] The author collaborated with John Sheridan to refine this information. Mr. Sheridan agrees with the changes to his timeline presented here.
[55] Multiple versions of the Round badge exist, but all pre-date the introduction of labels. Multiple versions of the Square badge are described in the Badges Article.
[56] See Section VIII, Table 14.

Figure 8 Stop Sign Badge #3
(photo by Adam Willis)

Figure 9. Square Badge #2
(photo by Rob Cook)

    The changes in badge styles correlate very closely with the numerical progression of serial numbers. All RB drums fall into the First Sequence, with serial numbers ranging from about 1001 to about 117000. SSB#1, the initial Stop Sign badge, first appears at about serial number 117000 and finishes out the First Sequence through about number 136500. A small amount of overlap is seen at the transition, with some SSB#1 drums possessing serial numbers lower than 117000 and some RB drums possessing serial numbers higher than 117000. Some of the RB drums with serial numbers higher than 117000 appear to be altered.[57]

    In addition to using the last about 20,000 serial numbers in the First Sequence, SSB#1 badges continue through about serial number 72000 in the Second Sequence, for a total of about 92,000 drums. The first Square badge, SQB#1, begins there and continues from about serial number 72000 through about 82000, for a total of about 10,000 drums. SSB#2 appears from serial number 82000 through about 92000, for a total of about 10,000 drums.[58] SSB#3 takes over at about 98000 and continues through about 125000, for a total of about 27,000 drums. SQB#2 starts at about 125000, finishes out the Second Sequence and starts the Third.

    As Sheridan points out, Round badges are tacked onto mounted toms and floor toms while small grommets attach vented badges on snare drums and larger grommets are used for bass drums. Uniformity in the form of vented badges with 3/8" grommets for all types of drums starts with the introduction of the SSB#1 style badge. Even if a badge is missing, the existence and size of a vent hole in a Gretsch drum may still provide information. A vent hole is an indicator that a tom is not from the Round badge era. Similarly, a large (17/32") vent hole in the top of the bass drum indicates that a missing badge was Round.

---

[57] Many partial drums, stripped shells, rewrapped drums which are described by their owners as RB drums fall into this group.
[58] A gap exists between serial numbers 92000 and 98000 in the Second Sequence. This corresponds with the transition from SSB#2 to SSB#3. Whether the labels are missing or just missing from the log is not clear. Because some SSB#2 drums have serial numbers above 98000 and a few SSB#3 drums have serial numbers below 92000, it is suspected that a block of 6000 serial numbers was not used.

There is significant confusion regarding exactly when badge styles changed and how long multiple styles of badges were sold together. Many "mixed badge" sets exist which sport pairings of RB and SSB#1, SSB#1 and SQB#1, or combinations of SSB#2, SSB#3 and SQB#2 badges. Many theories for mixed badge sets are offered. Pairings of available inventory at the factory or at the music store are both possible, as badge style was likely not a significant factor when putting together a set, like size and finish. In particular, the change from RB to SSB#1 is only made murkier by the 1971 Catalog. The cover pictures drums with both styles of badges. Inside the catalog, some of the marching drums have Round badges, while all other drums sport SSB#1 badges. Similar confusion surrounds the 1981 catalog, which pictures three different badge styles – SQB#1, SSB#2, and SSB#3.

One significant phenomenon is that SQB#1 was introduced before rather than after SSB#2 as previously presented by Egart and Sheridan. This conclusion is supported by multiple observations. First is the overlapping of serial numbers. There is overlap in the serial numbers transitioning from SSB#1 to SQB#1, SQB#1 to SSB#2, and then again from SSB#2 to SSB#3. There is no overlap from SSB#2 to SQB#1 or SQB#1 to SSB#3.[59] Also, many mixed badge factory matched sets appear in combinations which tend to support the earlier introduction of the SQB#1 badge.[60] Further support is provided when one looks at the changes in label styles in the next section.

> **Square Badge #1 was introduced before, not after, Stop Sign Badge #2.**

The timing of the use of the SQB#1 badge is the only major difference between the Sequential Serial Number system presented in this article and the information presented by Egart in 1984 and John Sheridan in recent articles. After exchanging correspondence with the author about the serial number information that collected in the log, John Sheridan agreed that the SQB#1 badge was used before the SSB#2.[61]

In addition to SQB#1, some of the other badge introduction dates suggested by Egart and Sheridan appear to be inconsistent with the log. It appears that the SSB#3 was not as short-lived as Egart and Sheridan suggest. Approximately 27,000 drums have that badge, more than SQB#1 and SSB#2 combined, which each had a run of about 10,000. Yet, the Egart/Sheridan timelines indicate that SSB#3 was in use for less than a year. A

---

[59] For example, there are a few SSB#1 drums with serial numbers above 72350, which is when SQB#1 drums appear in the log. Likewise, there is one SQB#1 drum with a serial number above 82250, which is when the SSB#2 badge first appears. If the labels were simply used out of sequence, i.e.: one roll of labels from 72250 to 82250 was misplaced and used later, the overlap at the transition points would not present itself in this manner. The transition between SSB#2 and SSB#3 is muddled somewhat by the lack of labels between 92000 and 98000, but as described in the prior note, some SSB#3 appear before 92000 and some SSB#2 appear after 98000. Since SQB#2 does not appear until about serial number 125000 (and sporting a different type of label as will be discussed in the next section), there is likely no confusion between the two versions of the Square badges.

[60] Although the number of reliable reports of factory mixed badge sets is not large, these sets tend to be combinations of RB/SSB#1, SSB#1/SQB#1, SQB#1/SSB#2, SSB#2/SSB#3, and SSB#3/SQB#2. There do not seem to be SSB#1/SSB#2 mixed badge sets reported.

[61] Sheridan indicated that his estimate of the introduction of SQB#1 was influenced by Egart's Centennial Article. Mr. Egart could not be located to determine if he concurs with the adjustment.

production volume of 27,000 in one year is not consistent with the overall volume seen during this time period. Although one should be somewhat cautious about suggesting changes to the framework for the late 1970s and early 1980s when an article published in 1984 should contain the timeliest and most reliable information, adjustments appear to be justified. These adjustments cannot be made without additional study of the other changing characteristics, which follows. Sheridan indicated to me that the timeline presented in the Badges Article relied upon Egart's. Sheridan agrees with the adjustments to the timeline which are presented here.

> **The Drop G Badge (SSB#3) was in use for about three year and not as rare as the Gretsch timeline indicates.**

Charting badge styles and serial numbers together provides some insight into the progression of badges and serial numbers through time.

Table 2
Badge Style and Serial Number
© Richard E. Gier 2011, 2023

Badge Style	Approximate Serial Number Range
RB	First Sequence 1001 - 117000
SSB#1	First Sequence 117000 - 136500 & Second Sequence 00001 - 72000
SQB#1	Second Sequence 72000 - 82000
SSB#2	Second Sequence 82000 - 92000
NONE MADE	Second Sequence 92000 - 98000
SSB#3	Second Sequence 98000 - 125000
SQB#2	Second Sequence 125000 - 148500 & Third Sequence 19780 - up

3.   Label Style.

Gretsch used a total of four different styles of labels during the twenty plus years spanned in this research.

   a.   <u>Orange/White with Shell Guarantee ("OW1")</u>. The first label introduced is orange and white with black printing. It contains the Gretsch lifetime shell guarantee which is first mentioned in the 1961 catalog. The OW1 label is used for the entire First Sequence, accounting for about 135,500 drums. The OW1 label is also used for about the first 51,600 serial numbers in the Second Sequence, although a few numbers above this are recorded. Therefore, approximately 187,100 drums have OW1 labels.[62] All labeled RB drums and the majority of SSB#1 drums have OW1 labels. The last 500 or so (serial

---

[62] There is no telling how many labels were damaged or discarded during the production process. If an error was made, a label may have been discarded and replaced rather than marking through the mistake. Note that if every drum had a label, and some labels were discarded, then the overall production volumes considered in this paper will be overstated by the number of discarded labels. Although they are not plentiful, a few labels with strike-throughs have been found.

numbers 51100 – 51600) of the main group of OW1 labels had the guarantee language removed by cutting the label into three pieces (top 1/3, middle 1/6 and bottom 1/2), discarding the middle portion and splicing together the top and bottom portions to make a version of the OW1 label without the guarantee language. This "Spliced OW1" label was so short lived that it is not designated as a separate label style.[63] This introduces Gretsch's intention to excise its lifetime shell guarantee from its labels. As will be supported later in this guide, this happened in about 1975.

      b.   <u>Orange/White Without Shell Guarantee – The Recut OW1 ("OW2")</u>. Gretsch's second label style is the OW1 label with the label cut in such a way that the model and serial number moved to the top and the guarantee language is removed. An OW2 label therefore is the bottom third of one OW1 label still attached to the top half of the next, with the remaining one-sixth containing the guarantee cut off. The cuts were not precise, so some labels are cut at an angle and different amounts of the black dot are visible at what is now the top of the label. The OW2 label is not as tall as the OW1 label, because the guarantee language was cut off.

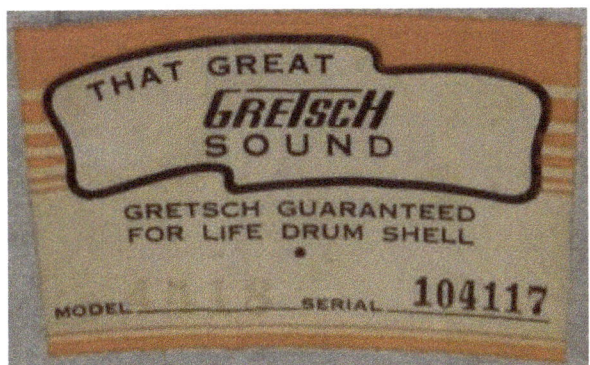

Figure 10. OW1 Label
(photo by author)

Figure 11. OW2 Label
(photo by Bill Maley)

     Some early OW2 labels have perforations very evident between the model/serial number at the top and the "Gretsch" logo at the bottom, where it would be for an OW1 label. Later OW2 labels are perforated at top and bottom, where appropriate for the OW2 label. These later OW2 labels may have been truly redesigned labels, not just recut OW1 labels, but that is not certain. There are only a small number of OW1 labels which have higher serial numbers than the lowest known serial number which appear on OW2 labels. There are no known duplicate numbers between OW1 and OW2 labels from the Second Sequence.

     Some have speculated that the switch from OW1 to OW2 labels, and importantly the discontinuation of the lifetime guarantee language, occurred when Baldwin purchased Gretsch in 1967. While at first blush this is an attractive explanation, it appears that the switch to the OW2 label occurred about eight years later.

---

[63] Serial numbers 51143, 51214, 51215, 51216 and 51656 all have spliced together OW1 labels.

> **The removal of the Lifetime Shell Guarantee language from the labels does not coincide with the sale of Gretsch to Baldwin in 1967.**

The OW2 label was used for serial numbers from about 51600 to about 75000 in the Second Sequence, but not 66000 to 68000. There are about 21,400 OW2 labels. OW2 labels appear on drums with SSB#1 and SQB#1 badges. An occasional drum with a Round Badge and an OW2 label appears on eBay. These drums usually show evidence of alterations or are from sellers with less than stellar reputations, so they are believed to not be authentic original drums.

    c.   <u>Orange/White with Guarantee Blacked Out ("Blacked Out OW1")</u>. For some unknown reason, Gretsch returned to using OW1 labels but blacked out the guarantee language with magic marker rather than removing it.[64] Almost every reported label in the 66000-68000 serial number range of the Second Sequence has blacked out guarantee language.[65] This serial number range is well above the transition point between OW1 and OW2 labels. It appears that these OW1 labels were not cut to create OW2 labels. Instead of scissors or a knife, the guarantee language was removed with a marker. Based upon an original owner report, a drum with an OW1 label with the guarantee blacked out was purchased in December 1977, so that helps to place this in time.

Figure 12. OW1 with Guarantee Blacked Out
(photo by Bill Maley)

Figure 13. OW3 Label
(photo by author)

    d.   <u>Orange/White without Shell Guarantee – Redesigned ("OW3")</u>. A third label, the second version of the Orange and White label without the guarantee, varies from the OW2 label. Sheridan did not note two variations of the orange and white label with no guarantee in his Badges Article, grouping OW2 and OW3 together in one category. Therefore, the existence of the OW3 label is introduced here. It appears that

---

[64] Recorded examples of OW1 labels with Blacked Out Guarantee language are serial numbers 61257, 64932, 66012, 66036, 66089, 66090, 66100, 66139, 66166, 66176, 66249, 66277, 64932, 66249, 66277, 66403, 66513, 66667, 66903, 66922, 66993, 67055, 67061, 67065, 67069, 67153, 67334, 67348, 67429, 67445, 67448, 67453, 67469, 67600, 67609, 67632, 67729, 67808, 67851 67956 and 67966. Others undoubtedly exist.

[65] Thirty-eight of forty entries have been confirmed to have the blacked out guarantee language. Information is not available on the other two entries, which were recorded prior to 2008 and before the phenomenon was recognized.

Gretsch tired of recutting OW1 labels, or simply used up their supply of OW1 labels, so a new design was created. The OW3 label is shorter than the OW2 label and has a different design than the OW1 and OW2 labels. The OW3 label lacks a thin orange line above the "That Great Gretsch Sound" banner just below the model and serial number lines and has one fewer pair of orange/white lines near the bottom of the banner. The banner portion of the OW3 label is more compressed than the banner used in the OW1/OW2 design. Many OW3 labels appear to have been perforated at top and bottom for easy tearing, although it is often difficult to detect perforations in pictures of labels. The switch from OW2 to OW3 labels occurs at about 75000 in the Second Sequence. OW3 labels are used from about 75000 to 90000 in the Second Sequence, accounting for about 15,000 labels. OW3 labels appear on SQB#1 and SSB#2 badges. No overlap is noted at the transition from OW2 to OW3 labels, which is expected if the new labels were ordered to start when the old ones left off.

  e. <u>Gray/White Label ("GW1")</u>. The fourth label is Gray and White with black printing. It is smaller than the OW1 and OW2 labels and about the same size as OW3. Drums with GW labels sport SSB#3 and SQB#2 badges. The GW1 label appears during the Second Sequence at about serial number 90000 and continues up to about 143000.

  f. <u>Gray/White Label ("GW2")</u>. The fifth label is also Gray and White with black printing. This second style of GW badge debuted at serial number 143000 and continued in the Second Sequence to 148500. This label continues in use into the Third Sequence, starting at about 20000 and continuing from there. Drums with GW labels sport SQB#2 badges. GW2 is much like the first style GW1, but now there is a gray border around the white box on the right half of the label. In addition, the serial number now is printed with a dot matrix printer. Rob Cook located a Gretsch internal memo dated September 19, 1983, addressing the change from label style GW1 to GW2, so we have an approximate date for the change. Very little data is collected on the drums of the Third Sequence, particularly after about serial number 60000. These drums won't be "vintage" for another decade or more and are not the focus of this paper.

Unlike the transition from OW1 to OW2, the transitions from OW3 to GW1 and then GW1 to GW2 labels were clean and absolute. There is no overlap in serial numbers between the different styles of labels. When changes in the label style were made, the serial number sequence continued uninterrupted.

Figure 14. GW1 Label
(photo by Rob Cook)

Figure 15. GW2 Label
(photo by Bill Maley)

g. <u>Mixed Label Sets</u>. Several drum sets exist today which appear to have been originally sold as sets but have more than one label style. This is certainly understandable, as the wrap or finish would be the primary factor in putting together sets, whether at the factory or the retail store, and little if any regard was likely given to the label type. Several sets possessing pairings of OW1 & OW2 and OW3 & GW1 labels seem to exist, but no verifiable reports of original factory sets with a combination of OW1 & GW1 labels have been observed.[66]

h. <u>Label Changes and the Badge Timeline</u>. One should tread carefully when challenging the long-established badge timeline provided by Egart and Sheridan. However, as discussed above in the badges section, there are many reasons to question the timing of the introduction of the SQB#1 badge. In addition to the factors already addressed, the progression of label styles lends further support for moving the SQB#1 in front of the SSB#2 in the timeline.

Throughout the period covered here - 1960s-early 1980s - Gretsch badge styles change at different times than the label styles. There is always overlap as the badges stay the same and the labels change, and vice versa. Many different pairings of badges and labels exist. The nature of the changes of label styles strongly supports the theory that the SQB#1 badge was introduced before the SSB#2 badge. Although there is a possibility that some rolls of labels were used out of order for SQB#1 drums, it seems highly unlikely that such out-of-order rolls involved both OW2 labels, which were recut OW1 labels, and OW3 labels, which are redesigned and used as printed.

i. <u>Summary of Characteristics Analyzed Thus Far</u>. The following table summarizes the characteristics discussed thus far: Serial Number, Badge Style and Label Style. A great deal of information about a drum can be gleaned from just these three pieces of information.

---

[66] Since the distinction between OW2 and OW3 labels is a new one, insufficient information exists to determine if OW2/OW3 mixed label sets exist.

Table 3
Badge Style, Label Style & Serial Number
© Richard E. Gier 2011, 2023

Badge Style	Label Style	Approximate Serial Number Range
RB	OW1	First Sequence 1001 – 117000
SSB#1	OW1	First Sequence 117000 – 136500 Second Sequence 00001 – 51600
SSB#1	OW2	Second Sequence 51600 – 72000
SSB#1	OW1 Blacked Out Guarantee	Second Sequence 66000 – 68000
SSB#1	OW2	Second Sequence 68000 – 72000
SQB#1	OW2	Second Sequence 72000 – 75000
SQB#1	OW3	Second Sequence 75000 – 82000
SSB#2	OW3	Second Sequence 82000 – 90000
SSB#2	GW1	Second Sequence 90000 – 92000
SSB#3	GW1	Second Sequence 98000 – 125000
SQB#2	GW1	Second Sequence 125000 – 143000
SQB#2	GW2	Second Sequence 143000 – 148500 Third Sequence 20000 – up

4. **Model Number.**

Model numbers appear in Gretsch's catalogs long before they are placed on the drums themselves. Once the labels appear, space is provided on the label for the model number. Gretsch model numbers are largely constant over time. For example, model 4416 was used on 9x13 two headed, separate tension toms for decades. Even when toms get deeper in the 1980s, model 4416 is still associated with 13 inch diameter, double headed, separate tension toms, even with the depth increasing to 11 or 13 inches. As evident in catalogs, particularly in the 1970s and 1980s, more tom diameters became available, so new model numbers are added. Also, as time passed, simple four digit model numbers are appended with additional letters and numbers like "W" for wood finish, "R" for rosewood, "M" for magnum (power depth) and "MS" for magnum square (diameter equal to depth). Additional letters appear in front of the familiar four digit codes as well.

This paper does not attempt to extensively analyze the progression of model numbers. One need only review copies of the catalogs to track the model numbers used by Gretsch. Changes in model numbers and the emergence of new model numbers over time permit a rough correlation to be made to the catalogs in which the model numbers first appear. Model numbers by themselves serve as helpful reference points for comparison of other characteristics. Model numbers collected here serve several purposes. First, they act as surrogates for drum sizes when measurements are not provided. Second, they verify dimensions which are given or permit reasonable adjustments where inexperienced sellers measure drums incorrectly, i.e.: a 13.5 inch diameter, 10 inch depth, model 4416, RB drum is assumed to be a 9x13. Third, as later described, the manner in which Gretsch provides model numbers on its labels changes over time, providing additional useful information. Fourth, two headed drums which left the factory as concert toms and are later converted are often discovered by their concert tom model numbers. The origin of other drums which are cut down from their factory sizes are also revealed by looking at their original model numbers.

5. Model Number – Stamped, Handwritten or Blank.

Initially, model numbers are stamped onto the OW1 labels with rubber stamps. This practice of stamped model numbers continues through the entire First Sequence and into the Second Sequence. This practice covers all RB drums and the first of the SSB#1 drums. Handwritten model numbers then became the norm starting at about serial number 22000 in the Second Sequence. The transition between stamped and handwritten model numbers appears somewhat abrupt. There are few stamped model numbers above serial number 22000 and few handwritten ones below it. The existence of many blank model numbers makes the moment of transition difficult to pinpoint. OW2, OW3 and GW labels have handwritten model numbers. Examples of stamped and handwritten model numbers can be seen in the labels shown as Figures 1-3, 10-13 and 15.

Some stamps were lightly applied or are difficult to see in pictures. In other cases, inks are faded or labels are water damaged or torn, leaving faint indication of model number. Other labels appear to have never had model numbers on them.[67] Reports of blank model numbers are infrequent on RB drums in the first half of the First Sequence. Blank model numbers seem more prevalent above serial number 70000 of the First Sequence, and during the Second Sequence, occurring during both the stamped and the handwritten periods. In particular, the first 20,000 labels in the Second Sequence, when stamped model numbers are expected, contain a significant number of blank model numbers.[68]

Knowing nothing but whether a model number is handwritten or stamped can actually be very useful in estimating a drum's age. All stamped model numbers are on OW1 labels, but not all OW1 labels have stamped model numbers, as the practice of stamping model numbers stopped during the time that the OW1 label was used. If the model number is stamped onto an OW1 label, the drum is older than a drum that has a handwritten model number on an OW1 label. If the serial number is above 22000 and the model number is stamped, it is likely a RB badge drum and the serial number is from the First Sequence. If one has an OW1 label with a serial number above 22000 and the model number is handwritten, then the drum is from the Second Sequence and originally had a SSB#1 badge. Serial numbers below 22000 from both the First and Second Sequences have stamped model numbers, so the labels from drums with these serial numbers look the same and the existence of a stamped model number provides no guidance. However, even though they may both be stamped, serial numbers 1000-7000 of the First Sequence can be distinguished from the same range of serial numbers in the

---

[67] Where no evidence of a model number could be seen on a label, that drum was treated as if the model number had been left blank. This category may include faded numbers and water damaged and torn labels.
[68] Compounding the analysis is that for a significant period, it was not noted in the log whether the model number was stamped or handwritten, leaving some gaps in the available data.

Second Sequence by the lack of leading zeros. If the model number is blank, there is nothing definitive one can say, as blank model numbers appeared throughout the history of labels.

Table 4
Stamped vs. Handwritten Model Numbers on OW1 Labels
© Richard E. Gier 2011, 2023

Badge Style	Approximate Serial Number Range	Model Number
RB	First Sequence 1001 – 7000*	Stamped
RB	**First Sequence 07000 – 22000 ****	**Stamped**
RB	First Sequence 22000 – 117000	Stamped
SSB#1	First Sequence 117000 – 136500	Stamped
SSB#1	Second Sequence 00001 – 07000***	Stamped
SSB#1	**Second Sequence 07000 – 22000 ****	**Stamped**
SSB#1	Second Sequence 22000 – 51600	Handwritten

* No leading zeros up to at least serial number 7000 in First Sequence.
** Labels with stamped model numbers and serial numbers 07000 – 22000 could be from either the First or Second Sequence.
*** Leading zeros from 00001 through about 09999 during SSB#1 era.

6. Model Number – Color of Ink.

As Sheridan points out in his Badges Article, Gretsch changes the color of ink it uses to indicate the model number.[69] Initially, the model number is stamped in black ink. This continues exclusively in black ink until around serial number 36000 of the First Sequence. Both black and blue inks are used above this serial number, with no apparent preference for one color over another and no long periods when one color is exclusive. It seems as if a new blue ink pad is purchased and blue and black are both used.[70] The use of both colors of ink continues as long as serial numbers are stamped onto labels, including all of the First Sequence and the first part of the Second Sequence.

When model numbers begin to be handwritten at around serial number 22000 in the Second Sequence, Gretsch uses Green markers almost exclusively. Black and Blue markers occasionally appear, but green dominates the Second Sequence from about serial number 22000 until about serial number 90000 and then all but disappears. After this point, black marker dominates for the remainder of the Second and Third Sequences, with blue, an occasional red and orange model number observed. Ink pens are used at times in lieu of markers, particularly in the Third Sequence.

---

[69] After reading the Badges article, the author added ink color to the data collected.
[70] Early in the Second Sequence, two labels display handwritten red ink model numbers where the word "special" is indicated (serial numbers 02373 and 02736). One has only the word "Special" while the other has "Special 13x10". This was before the switch from stamped to handwritten model numbers. It appears that although Gretsch possessed a "Special" stamp which is used on some special-order drums, "special" was handwritten on others. One collector reports an SSB#2 14x16 factory bass drum with "special" written in green ink and a 26" bass drum with "Special" stamped in black ink.

Color of ink provides some insight into the age of a drum, but as colors come and go and sometimes reappear, ink color is not a characteristic which provides definitive proof of the age of a drum. At best, ink color tends to provide support of what other characteristics indicate.

Table 5
Ink Color Used for Model Numbers
© Richard E. Gier 2011, 2023

Approximate Serial Number Range	Model Number	Ink Color
First Sequence 1001 – 36000	Stamped	Black
First Sequence 36000 – 136500	Stamped	Black / Blue
Second Sequence 00001 – 22000	Stamped	Black / Blue
Second Sequence 22000 – 90000	Handwritten	Green / Black / Blue
Second Sequence 90000 – 148500	Handwritten	Black / Blue
Third Sequence 20000 – Up	Handwritten	Black / Blue

7. Model Number – Size and Font

The size and font used for Gretsch model number stamps changed over time.[71] About the first 500 serial numbers in the First Sequence (1001 –1500) used a Large Digit stamp.[72] Then, for the remainder of the First Sequence, a Regular Digit was used for all drums - except a brief reprise of the Large Digit stamp in the 118101-118702 serial number range. This Regular Digit stamp appeared into the Second Sequence. Early in the Second Sequence the font changed. It is most easily distinguished by an open four, as seen in Figure 3, replacing a closed four. This open font was used until about serial number 22000 in the Second Sequence when stamping of model numbers ceased.

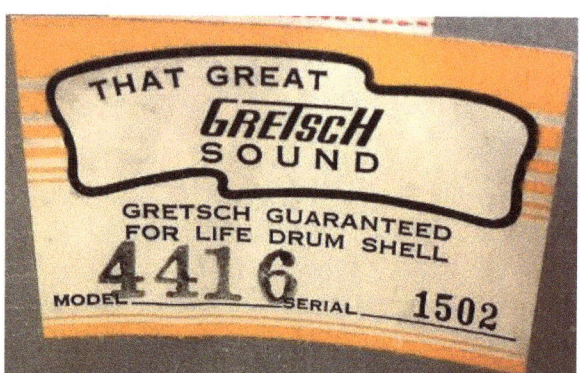

Figure 16. Large Digit Model Number
(Photo by David Dudley, Dave's Drum Shop)

---

[71] Richard E. Gier, "Model Numbers in Vintage Gretsch Drums," February 28, 2022. Available at www.gretschdrumdatingguide/other projects and https://www.notsomoderndrummer.com/not-so-modern-drummer/2022/2/25/model-numbers-in-vintage-gretsch-drums

[72] The Large Digit model numbers made a brief reprise just after the Stop Sign Badge was introduced. About 600 drums with serial numbers 118101-118702 received model numbers stamped with Large Digits model numbers. Interestingly, these were not the Stop Sign Badge drums with the lowest serial numbers, as the badge switch occurred at about serial number 117000. Once again, it is not clear why Gretsch briefly switched back to the Large Digit stamps or why this block of 600 drums was selected to receive them.

8. Lug Casing Attachment Screw Head Type – Round or Hexagonal.

Gretsch used round head screws to attach its lug casings to its shells for many years before it began to apply paper labels inside its drums. In the late 1960s, Gretsch abandoned the round head screws in favor of hexagonal ("hex") head screws. Sheridan mentions the screw head type in his Badges Article, indicating that earlier 1960s drums had round heads and the later 1960s drums had hex heads. This change occurred in the 96000 serial number range in the First Sequence. This likely occurred in the 1967-1968 time frame. The transition was not sudden, as many drums with higher serial numbers sport round screws and some with lower numbers have hex heads. This gradual transition might be explained by the need to use up factory inventory. An additional explanation is suggested. Of all the characteristics addressed thus far, this seems the easiest to alter. Some alterations may be innocent, as few needing lugs for a shell or replacement screws for their stripped self-tapping hex head screws would likely give much thought to the screw head type. Some alterations may be less innocent, as a relatively easy way to make a drum look "older" is to use round head screws rather than hex head ones.

The inability to differentiate between First and Second Sequence serial numbers between 07051 and 22000 on OW1 labels noted in Table 5 is easily resolved if one looks at the screw head type. First Sequence serial numbers in that range have round heads while Second Sequence serial numbers in the same range have hexagonal heads. This tip may be helpful in situations where badges are missing, badge tack or vent holes are not apparent on toms, or badge grommets appear to be tampered with on snare drums.

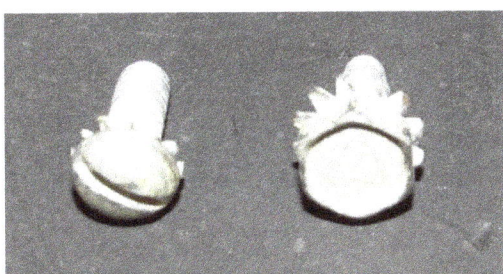

Figure 17. Round and Hexagonal Head Attachment Screws
(photo by author)

There has been some speculation that the switch from round to hex head screws occurred when Gretsch moved its production from Brooklyn, NY, to Booneville, Arkansas, in the late 1960s, after the sale of the company to Baldwin Music Company. This much is known: Baldwin bought Gretsch in 1967 and production was moved to Booneville, Arkansas in 1969 or 1970.[73] Other than speculation and roughly coincidental

---

[73] In July 2008 during a promotional event at Explorer's Drums in Kansas City, Missouri, the author asked Fred W. Gretsch when the factory moved from Brooklyn to Booneville. He responded that it occurred in 1969. Falzerano interviewed Duke Kramer and Bill Hagner who indicate other dates for the move to Arkansas. Falzerano, p. 67, 68. John Sheridan has spoken with Brooklyn Gretsch employees who indicated that they worked there until 1970, but another who placed the move in the summer of 1969. Email correspondence with John Sheridan, November 8, 2010.

timing, no definitive link between the change in screw heads type and these events has been identified. Even without linking the head type change to the move to Arkansas, we can generally conclude that an original drum with round head screws was manufactured in or before 1968, while one with hex head screws was made in or after 1967.

It should be noted that the screw head type on other hardware appears to have changed at a different time. There are many examples of floor toms with round head screws attaching the lug casings and hex head screws attaching the floor tom leg mounts. The type of screws for floor tom mounts is not recorded. Some slotted hex head screws begin to appear in the 66000 serial number range.

Table 6
Type of Head on Lug Casing Attachment Screws
© Richard E. Gier 2011, 2023

Approximate Serial Number Range	Screw Head Type
First Sequence 1001 – 96000	Round
First Sequence 96000 – 136500	Hexagonal
Second Sequence 00001 – 148500	Hexagonal
Third Sequence 20000 – Up	Hexagonal

9. **Wrap/Finish.**

Certain wraps and finishes (together referred to here as "finish") are offered unchanged for decades. Others are introduced and/or discontinued, at least according to the finish charts in the catalogs, at roughly known times. Because of the gradual phasing in and out of various finishes, one cannot date a Gretsch drum simply by its finish. There appear to be at most a correlation between the dates a finish is shown in catalogs and the availability of that finish to a buyer. Much internet forum discussion and many anecdotal comments put a rough range of availability of a finish three years before it appears and three years after it disappears from a catalog. This range may be even larger, depending upon the frequency of production of catalogs and the supply of particular finishes. Therefore, finishes are generally not a very precise tool for determining a date range for a Gretsch drum. However, if serial numbers were issued sequentially, then one might expect to see certain finishes appear and disappear in a manner consistent with the progression of serial numbers. This generally is observed with a large number of different finishes, discussed below.[74]

Anniversary Sparkle was offered to commemorate Gretsch's 75th anniversary in 1958. Many anecdotal accounts indicate that this wrap was still available well into the 1960s, although it did not appear in catalogs of that era. Eventually, the supply of such a

---

[74] Note that serial number ranges listed for the emergence and disappearance of particular finishes are based upon drums recorded in the log and are not believed to be precise. The log contains only a small percentage of the drums produced. Because of the large number of finishes, the link of finish to serial numbers is only a rough one. Nonetheless, it provides some additional support for the use of serial numbers in rough sequential order.

wrap would be depleted. Anniversary Sparkle wrap drums only appear in the lower serial numbers of the First Sequence, with the highest reported drum in the 16000 range.

The Satin Flame finishes first appeared in a June 22, 1965 price list and the 1966 catalog, but are believed to have been available for at least a few years before then. The lowest serial number in the log for a satin flame finish drum is in the 13000 range in the First Sequence for a Silver Satin Flame set. With higher serial numbers, the frequency of more colorful satin flame offerings, like moonglow and red, increased. Satin Flame finishes are not currently recorded above serial number 25000 in the Second Sequence. Brushed aluminum finish snares (models 4105, 4106, 4108 and 4109)[75] first appear in the March 1, 1969 Retail Price List and at about serial number 73000 in the First Sequence. The lack of brushed aluminum finish drums below that serial number range is consistent with a late 1960s introduction of the finish.

Two short-lived finishes, Emerald Green Pearl and Red Wine Pearl, appear only in the 1971 catalog and in the log in the highest RB and the lowest SSB#1 serial number ranges (115000 to 135000 in the First Sequence). This is consistent with the wraps being offered only in the very late 1960s and early 1970s, when the badges were being changed from RB to SSB#1. In addition, Chrome over Wood first appears in the 1971 supplement catalog and the 04000 range of the Second Sequence.

As Gretsch moved toward non-wrapped drums, one would expect wood finished drums to be more prevalent in the later serial numbers. Although this point is subjective because many drums have been stripped of a wrap and refinished, the log contains very few RB badge drums with a factory wood finish.[76] This makes sense, as the wood finishes grew in popularity in the 1970s, after the RB was discontinued. The first mentions of the "Rich Walnut" finish are the March 1, 1969 retail price list and the 1969 catalog. Drums with wood finishes are much more prevalent in the SSB era than the RB era.

Although subject to exceptions, the time/serial number/finish relationship seems strong for the entire time frame considered in this paper. Although the strong correlation in the later years (1970s and 1980s) is not proof of a correlation in the 1960s RB era, it offers support that Gretsch issued its serial numbers in sequential order.

10. Two Headed vs. Concert Tom.

The vast majority of Gretsch drums in the time frame studied are two headed. Although some single headed, concert tom style drums were offered early on,[77] the vast

---

[75] Some early aluminum drums are labeled as model 4105 before model number 4108 came into use. Some early 4108 models are wrapped wood drums.

[76] Although several RB drums are observed with wood finishes, the owners generally describe them as having had their wraps removed or having been refinished or there are indications that the shells were wrapped at one time (visible seams and loose badge grommets). Some reliable reports of original walnut finished drums appear as low as the 103000 serial number range in the First Sequence.

[77] Chico Hamilton is pictured in advertisements with RB concert toms, but may have been one of the few who played them.

majority of concert toms appear in the 1970s and 1980s. The 1977 Catalog shows large concert tom sets.

While a very few RB single headed toms are recorded in the log, concert toms are generally drums with SSB#1 and later badge styles. Concert toms generally have serial numbers from the 54000 range in the Second Sequence and later. Some concert toms have been converted to two headed toms, but many can be distinguished by their model numbers if present on the labels. Where the label is missing, a rough determination may still be made based upon this characteristic.

11. Throwoff / Strainer Type for Snare Drums.

Gretsch made significant changes to its hardware infrequently. The same throwoffs and strainers appear in catalogs on particular models of drums for long periods of time. When changes are made, they tend to affect all models of drums and are relatively abrupt. Therefore, hardware can be a useful indicator of a drum's age.[78] The Renown throwoff/strainer is in constant use on the 4103 and 4105 model snare drums from before the first labels through about 120000 in the First Sequence. Student model 4108 snare drums sport either the Renown or the "Standard" from its introduction until about 120000 in the First Sequence.[79] Model 4157 and 4160 snare drums have Microsensitive throwoffs starting before serial numbers and proceeding through about serial number 90000 of the First Sequence. The first style of Lightning Strainer ("L1"), with the throw arm on the left side replaces the Microsensitive. The L1 throwoff appeared from 90000 in the First Sequence to about 23000 in the Second Sequence. The second style of Lightning throwoff ("L2") has a center throw arm and is in use from about 23000 in the Second Sequence. The L1 and L2 throwoffs first appear in the 1969 and 1977 catalogs, respectively. John Sheridan reports that the L1 throwoff is originally advertised in Downbeat in April 1968, but may have already been in use for a while.[80] Further Sheridan indicates that the L2 throwoff is first mentioned in the January 15, 1975 price list.

Many of the throws have distinctive mounting hole patterns, so even where a drum is missing a throwoff/strainer, there may still be some indication of the type of throwoff/strainer which was originally on the drum.

---

[78] Note that small modifications were made to some throws (i.e.: number of mounting points for the Renown strainer) and butt ends were also changed. These variations were not captured in the log.
[79] Model 4108 was originally assigned to a wrapped wood shell but later was applied exclusively to brushed aluminum student snares. The timing of the introduction of the Standard throwoff is uncertain.
[80] Email correspondence with John Sheridan, November 11, 2010.

Figure 18. Microsensitive Throwoff
(photo by Adam Willis)

Figure 19. Renown Throwoff
(photo by author)

Figure 20. Lightning #1 Throwoff
(photo by author)

Figure 21. Lightning #2 Throwoff
(photo by Adam Willis)

Table 7
Throwoff/Strainer Associated with Each Snare Model
© Richard E. Gier 2011, 2023

Model No.	Approximate Serial Number Range	Throwoff/Strainer
4157, 4160	First Sequence 1001 – 90000	Microsensitive
	First Sequence 90000 – 136500	L1
	Second Sequence 00001 – 23000	L1
	Second Sequence 23000 – on	L2
4103, 4105	First Sequence 1001 – 120000	Renown
4108	First Sequence 73000 – 136500 Second Sequence 00001 - on	Renown/Standard

12. Drum Dimensions.

Drum sizes change over time, with depths increasing and additional diameters, both smaller and larger, offered as sets grew from four pieces to as many as ten. The drum sizes relate very closely with the size-based model numbers discussed earlier. However, the timing of the introduction of new sizes and the absence of these sizes with low serial number labels fits with the general pattern of sequential serial numbers. The size acts as a surrogate for model number when the label is blank.

13. Set Configuration.

For drums reported as parts of complete or partial sets, the entire configuration of the set is recorded. This information provides some insight. First, serial numbers for sets which appear to be originally sold together often, but not necessarily, have tightly grouped serial numbers. Many sets have serial numbers which share several initial digits, often grouped within a few thousand numbers of each other. In the SSB era, many sets are reported which have sequential numbers for multiple drums in the set. Sequential numbered sets do not appear in the log in the RB era. However, some "original" sets have serial numbers which range considerably, with serial numbers which are tens of thousands of numbers apart. This is particularly true of RB sets. Explanations offered by vintage drum fans include: many early sets were purchased without floor toms, which were added later; some sets may have been put together at the factory or by drum dealers and music stores from available stock; individual drums may have been added at later dates; and others.

Second, particular set configurations may offer insight into their ages based upon availability based upon catalog description. This is not a particularly precise date predictor, as catalog depictions are not very definitive of when a particular configuration may have been available, either as a stock set or special order.

Set configuration provides some corroborating support for trends seen with other characteristics, but by itself is only mildly instructive.

14. Chrome Snares – Center Decorative Knurled Band.

Gretsch began offering chrome-plated model 4160 snare drums before or very early during the labeled drum era. The drums with the lowest serial numbers, through about 56000 in the First Sequence, have no center decorative band of knurled markings, while those with numbers above about 56000 in the First Sequence have a center located band of decorative knurled markings. Based upon the drums recorded in the log, the transition between the drums with and without the decorative knurled markings is almost absolute.[81] It should be noted that some later model 4160, 4165 and 4166 chrome snares, particularly in the SQB#2 era, vary on whether they have knurled bands.

---

[81] This characteristic was not originally part of the information collected, so there are several drums for which the presence or absence of knurling is not noted.

Figure 22. Center Knurled Band
(photo by author)

Table 8
Decorative Knurling on Chrome Snare Drums
© Richard E. Gier 2011, 2023

Approximate Serial Number Range	Knurling
First Sequence 1001 – 56000	None
First Sequence 56000 – 136500	Present
Second Sequence 00001 – 100000	Present
Second Sequence 100000 – 148500	Varies
Third Sequence 20000 – Up	Varies

B. Anomalies and Oddballs. Those involved in vintage drums acknowledge that there are drums which simply do not fit the patterns. These drums may have been special orders, the result of clearing out old inventories, the result of parts shortages, recipients of post-factory modifications or explained by one of numerous unrecorded events. For example, no one seems to understand what triggered when 14x14 floor toms received large or small lug casings. Also, despite the introduction of the interior silver sealer in the 1950s, drums with unpainted interiors appear much later in time.[82] Three examples of guitar/banjo labels used in drums have been recorded.[83] The anomalies are not even contained to drums, as several cut down OW1 labels have been discovered inside Gretsch guitars.[84] This paper does not attempt to explain every drum or guarantee

---

[82] A group of thirty-three drums with unpainted shells are reported in the Round Badge era (72234 through 75473 serial number range of the First Sequence). Richard E. Gier, "Mid 1960s Gretsch Round Badge Drums without Silver Sealer," January 2021. Available at https://www.gretschdrumdatingguide.com/other-projects.html and Not So Modern Drummer, January 31, 2021, https://www.notsomoderndrummer.com/not-so-modern-drummer/2021/1/28/mid-1960s-gretsch-round-badge-drums-without-silver-sealer

[83] Serial numbers 2066, 2086 and 2111 from a set of guitar labels which appear leftover from about 1966 were used on drums with SSB#1 badges in the early 1970s.

[84] Forty-seven different examples of guitars and banjos possessing drum labels and/or serial numbers from the drum serial number sequence have been documented. Their serial numbers range from 23003 to 26781. Email correspondence with Edward Ball from June 9, 2011 through March 19, 2023.

that every drum made fits patterns described here. Not all of them fit or can be easily explained. This paper focuses on the vast majority of drums which do seem to fit.

Figure 23. 60s era Drum without Silver Sealer
(photo by author)

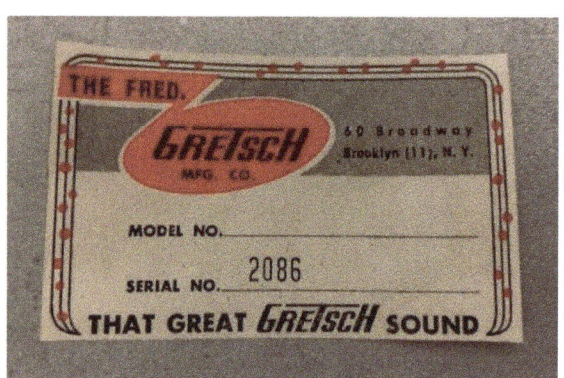

Figure 24. Guitar Label in 1970s era drum
(photo by Dave Michael)

Figure 25. Guitar Label in 1970s era drum
(photo by Pierre Van Craenenbroeck)

V. DATES LINKED TO GRETSCH DRUMS

A. Reports of Drums with Dates and Serial Numbers. Because the shells are not date-stamped like Ludwig or stamped with a month/year code like Slingerland, the estimation of Gretsch drums' ages is not precise.[85] However, there are several reports of original owner drums, some with original purchase receipts, and a number of secondary reports which were vetted and considered reliable. The number of reports of drums with reliable dates is not sufficient by itself to support the creation of an elaborate scheme to predict dates of Gretsch drums. These reports do however contribute to the dating guide when viewed in combination with other characteristics.

Table 9 shows reported date/serial number combinations which are considered highly reliable.

---

[85] Even with Ludwig there is at best a high correlation between serial numbers and dates.

Table 9
Reported Date/Serial Number Combinations Considered Highly Reliable
© Richard E. Gier 2011, 2023

Badge	Serial Number Sequence	Serial Number Range	Reported Purchase Date
RB	1st	1300 – 8200	November 21, 1962
RB	1st	4200 – 4500	November 1962
RB	1st	15000 - 17000	October 1963
RB	1st	23000 - 26000	August 1963
RB	1st	9100 - 9200	December 1963
RB	1st	33000 - 34000	April 1964
RB	1st	9000 & 37000	May 1964
RB	1st	38000 - 39000	April 1966
RB	1st	40000 & 47000	December 4, 1965
RB	1st	86000 - 87000	Late 1967
RB	1st	93000 – 95000	October 1967
RB	1st	76000 - 80000	December 1967
SSB#1	1st	116000 - 118000	September 1969
SSB#1	1st	117000 – 121000	December 1969
SSB#1	1st	122000 - 123000	December 1969
SSB#1	1st	132000 - 135000	October 23, 1971
SSB#1	1st	132000 - 135000	Early 1972
SSB#1	1st	135000 – 136000	December 1971 *
SSB#1	1st	129000 - 130000	1972**
SSB#1	2nd	04000 – 08000	December 1971 *
SSB#1	2nd	09000 – 12000	1972**
SSB#1	2nd	07000 - 08000	January 1972
SSB#1	2nd	16000 – 18000	December 17, 1973
SSB#1	2nd	11000 - 16000	October 14, 1974
SSB#1	2nd	59000 - 60000	October 1977
SSB#1	2nd	67000 - 68000	December 1977
SSB#1	2nd	52000 - 61000	November 22, 1979***
SQB#1	2nd	72000 - 73000	November 22, 1979***
SSB#3	2nd	101000 - 106000	September 1981
SSB#3	2nd	106000 - 126000	January 1982****
SQB#2	2nd	126000 - 130000	January 1982****
SQB#2	2nd	142000 -143000	Fall 1983
SQB#2	3rd	20000 - 21000	Sept/Oct 1984
SQB#2	3rd	48000 – 49000	August 1994

* These two entries involve a set with serial numbers from different Sequences.
** These two entries involve another set with serial numbers from different Sequences
*** These two entries involve a set with two different badge styles
**** These two entries involve a set with two different badge styles

Chart 1 graphically depicts the relationship between serial number and purchase date for the reports considered highly reliable.

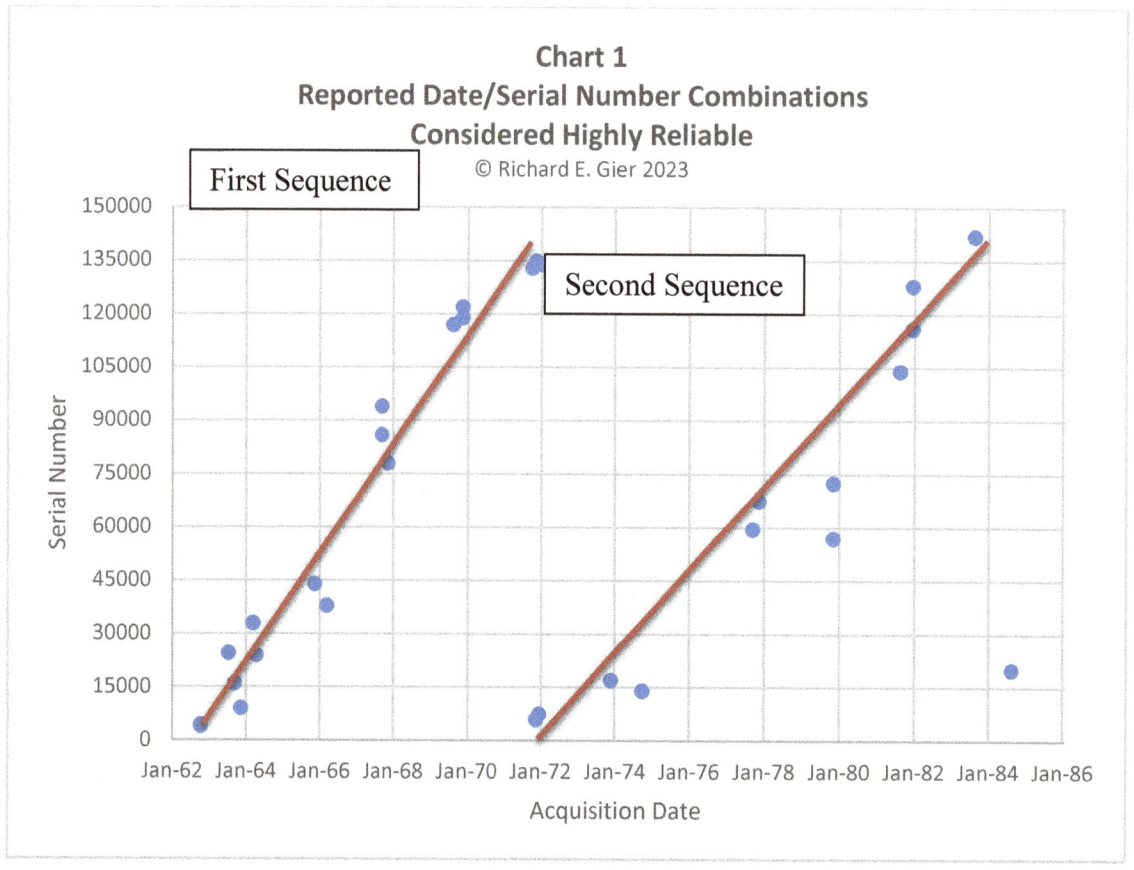

B. Linking Changing Physical Characteristics to Dates. The relatively small number of highly reliable reports of original purchase dates makes it difficult to tightly connect the information collected about physical characteristics, serial numbers and the dates that the drums were produced. This situation can be partially addressed by considering approximate dates for changes in specific physical characteristics. These dates can then be linked to the serial numbers associated with the changing physical characteristics. The ability to make this link requires an understanding of all of the changes that have been described above and the interrelationships of those changing characteristics.

Review of known dates or those which are widely regarded as reliable provides additional links between physical characteristics and manufacture dates. However, the link between the appearance and disappearance of characteristics in catalogs and the dates when the characteristics actually changed is somewhat tenuous. When the serial numbers where the changes occur are overlaid onto the dates of catalog or advertisements, additional insight is gained.

Table 10
Known Dates / Changes in Gretsch History
© Richard E. Gier 2011, 2023

Date and Source	Approximate Serial Number Range	Change in Physical Characteristic or Other Significant Event
1957 - 1963*	1001	Introduction of Labels (OW1)
1961 Catalog		Six-ply shells introduced
1963 Catalog #42		
1966 Catalog #43		Round Badges & Microsensitive throwoff 4160 Snares with and without knurling
	56000	Addition of knurling to 4160 Snare
1967		Gretsch sold to Baldwin
1968 Downbeat Ad		1st Ad showing L1 throw
	95000	Throw from Microsensitive to L1
	96000	Lug Screws from Round to Hex Head
1969 Catalog #44		Round Badges Only. "New" Lightning throw (L1) featured
1969 - 1970		Manufacturing moved to Arkansas
1971 - 1972**	117000	Badge from RB to SSB#1
1971 Catalog #45		Predominantly SSB#1 badge, some Round Badge. L1 throw is dominant, one drum features Microsensitive
	136500 1st Seq.	Serial Number Sequence to Second
1973		Plant Fires – January and December (1972 and 1973 per Egart)
	22000 2nd Seq.	Model No. from Stamp to Handwritten
1975 Price List		Introduction of L2 Throwoff
	23000	Throw from L1 to L2
	51100	Label to OW2
1977 Catalog		L2 throw pictured
1980**	**72000**	**Badge to SQB#1****
	75000	Label to OW3
Around 1979**	**82000**	**Badge to SSB#2****
	90000	Label to GW1
Early 1981**	92000/98000	Badge to SSB#3**
1981 Catalog		SQB#2, SSB#2 and SSB#3 all pictured
Late 1981**	125000	Badge to SQB#2**
September 1983	143000	Label to GW2
	148500 2nd Seq.	Serial Number Sequence to Third

* Range of dates based upon Sheridan's Badges Article, timeline on www.VintageDrumGuide.com, Maxwell vdf post, Falzerano and email exchanges with John Sheridan and Chet Falzerano.
** Range of dates for introduction of badge styles based upon Centennial and Badges Articles. Dates of badge introductions developed in this paper differ from those of Egart and Sheridan. See Section VII - Badge Timeline Revised for dates developed in this paper.

C. Can Serial Numbers Alone Be Used to Estimate Dates? Because of the numerous strong links between changing characteristics, serial numbers and the passage of time, it appears that serial numbers can be used as a date predictor. There is comfort that a cross-check of the predicted dates and the availability of changing wraps, finishes and hardware seems to fit the predictions. There is also comfort in taking a drum and seeing that it fits not only the patterns described above, but also fits within the picture that a vintage drum enthusiast has of the progression of styles, sizes, colors, etc.... through the decades. For example, a wood finish drum doesn't generally "belong" in the sixties. Likewise, neither do deep toms, concert toms and Tony Williams' yellow. Conversely, the Microsensitive throws don't generally "belong" on 70s or 80s drums.

Systematic analysis of over 8,600 serialized drums, including a small number of drums with fairly reliable original purchase dates, cross-checking against known dates of events and comparing to printed materials (catalogs, advertisements and price lists) used by Gretsch, and a certain amount of fitting the pieces together into a structure that works, creates **...drumroll please...**

VI. GRETSCH SERIAL NUMBER / DATE GUIDES

A. Round Badge Era:

Assumptions:

1. July 1, 1962 is the beginning date for the labels and serial numbers;[86]

2. July 1, 1969 is the last day for the Round Badge;

3. Round Badge serial numbers range from 1001 to 117000;

4. Production was not at a constant and even annual rate from mid-1962 to mid-1969. Years 1964-1967 were higher with 1966 being the peak year. This production estimate is based upon information conveyed to author by John Sheridan based upon his conversations with Gretsch employees.[87]

---

[86] For purposes of this paper 1962 is selected as the start date. It is possible that labels were introduced earlier and that lower production rates in the late 1950s and early 1960s would permit the earliest serial numbers to be spread out more during the early years. Additional reliable reports of labeled drums may shift this date in the future. In that event, production volume indicated during 1962 and 1963 may be redistributed to earlier years for a more gradual buildup of production in that period.
[87] Email correspondence with John Sheridan, November 8, 2010.

Table 11
Round Badge Serial Number Date Guide
© Richard E. Gier 2011, 2023

Year	Percentage of Total RB	Annual Production	Approximate Serial Number Range Start	Finish
1962	5 %	5,800	1001	6800
1963	10 %	11,600	6801*	18400
1964	15 %	17,400	18401	35800
1965	17 %	19,720	35801	55520
1966	20 %	23,200	55521	78720
1967	16 %	18,560	78721	97280
1968	12 %	13,920	97281	111200
1969	5 %	5,800	111201	117000

*Leading zeros appeared after about serial number 7050.

An Example: The author owns a RB Silver Glass Glitter Progressive Jazz set with a 14x20" bass drum with serial number 69711. It has an OW1 label with a blank model number. It has round head screws. Applying Sheridan's Rule alone points toward a mid-1960s date. According to the two guides above, it was most likely made around 1966. Absent the serial number, there are a few other characteristics which corroborate this date estimate. Because this finish and label style were available throughout the RB era, they provide no clues to the drum's date. The drum's size and the set configuration are also of no help, as those sizes were available for many years. In this particular case, the other drums in the set do not have serial numbers in the same range as the bass drum – it may be a set which was pieced together later – so that information is not helpful. The round head screws provide some assistance, as the switch from round head to hex head occurred in approximately the 1967-1968 time frame. The lack of a model number on the label is not conclusive. Absent the Dating Guide, our best estimate is a mid-1960s drum. With the Dating Guide, we are somewhat comfortable narrowing the estimate to about 1966.

B. Stop Sign / Square Badge Era:

The same approach can be applied to the Stop Sign Badge era. Although Round Badge drums were the original focus of the data collection effort, information on more than 4,400 Stop Sign and Square Badge drums was collected. Multiple badge changes, the timing of which is estimated in Sheridan's Badges Article, combined with multiple other changing physical characteristics, makes this era very intriguing. There are more original owner drums reported for this time frame which permits a greater number of specific serial numbers to be linked to specific dates.

Assumptions:

1. Production of SSB#1 drums began mid-year 1969 and ended near the beginning of 1977. A total of about 92,000 drums had SSB#1 badges. Serial numbers

ranged from 117000 to 136500 in the First Sequence and from 00001 to 72000 in the Second Sequence.

2. Production of SQB#1 drums began in about 1977 and ended in about 1978. A total of about 10,000 drums had SQB#1 badges. Serial numbers range from about 72000 to 82000 in the Second Sequence.

3. Production of SSB#2 Badge drums began in about 1978 and ended in about 1979. A total of about 10,000 drums had SSB#2 badges. Serial numbers range from about 82000 to 92000 in the Second Sequence.

4. Production of SSB#3 Badge drums began in about 1979 and continued through about the end of 1981. A total of about 27,000 drums had SSB#3 badges. Serial Numbers ranged from about 98000 to 125000 in the Second Sequence.

5. Production of the SQB#2 badge began in late 1981 or 1982. Serial Numbers started at about 125000 in the Second Sequence.

Table 12
Stop Sign/Square Badge Era Serial Number Date Guide
© Richard E. Gier 2011, 2023

Year	Badge Style	Production	Approximate Serial Number Range Start	Finish
1969	SSB#1	5800	117001 1st Seq.	122800 1st Seq.
1970	SSB#1	11000	122801	133800
1971	SSB#1	11000	134801 00001 2nd Seq.	136500 08300 2nd Seq.
1972	SSB#1	11000	08301	19300
1973	SSB#1	11000	19301	30300
1974	SSB#1	11000	30301	41300
1975	SSB#1	11000	41301	52300
1976	SSB#1	11000	52301	63300
1977	SSB#1/SQB#1	11000	63301	74300
1978	SQB#2/SSB#2	11000	74301	85300
1979	SSB#2/SSB#3	11000	85301*	102300*
1980	SSB#3	11000	102301	113300
1981	SSB#3	12000	113301	125300
1982	SQB#2	11000	125301	135300

* Lack of Reported Serial Numbers between 92000 – 98000.

An Example. The tom shell in the eBay ad which appears as the first listing displayed at the beginning of this article had the following characteristics: No badge, but has vent hole; 8x12 tom; no wrap; serial number 14665 on OW1 label; and blank model number. Everything but the seller's description points to a production date of about 1972. Despite the existence of a vent hole for the badge, the seller so wants this shell to be from the 1960s that they take Sheridan's Rule and misapplies it to the SSB era drum.

A Second Example. The Blue Sparkle floor tom in the second eBay ad displayed at the beginning of this article had the following characteristics: SSB#1 badge, 16x16 floor tom, Blue Glass Glitter wrap, serial number 122456 on OW1 label, model number 4418 stamped in blue ink, hex head screws. A review of earlier entries on the log revealed that the drum had been offered on eBay months before as part of a RB/SSB1 mixed set by a different seller. Everything but the seller's description points to a 1969/1970 production date. Early 60s? – No. Late 1960s/Early 70s? – Yes.

Another Example. A June 2009 eBay ad states: "Vintage Gretsch round badge era tom. 9 x 13. Silver interior. Has tag. Model# 4416. Serial# 80386. This has extra holes and an area cut out that must have been for a different mount. This is missing the badge. Has been painted a dark green." Pictures show a stripped shell with OW3 label, a handwritten model number with non-determinable ink color, holes for ball-style mount, and a vent hole for a badge. Based upon the guide, this drum dates to about 1978 and likely had an SQB#1 badge. This conclusion is supported by the OW3 label, the handwritten model number, the mount hole, and the vent hole for badge, as RB toms were not vented.

Yet Another Example. Suppose you find a 5x14 Gretsch 8 lug snare drum with no badge, a silver interior, and no label. The wrap has been removed and the drum appears to be refinished in a walnut stain. There are no extra holes. There is not much to work with to date this drum. However, you should look at whether the lug screws are round or hex heads. Also, look at the type of throwoff or holes for the throwoff and butt end. Certain styles were available during certain time frames. Realize that a drum in this condition could have been subject to other modifications, so you cannot be certain of anything on this drum. Even if you cannot determine when it was made, you can still enjoy the drum!

C. All Together Now.

Much of the information is gathered together into one master guide to assist in cross checking characteristics, particularly when not all of the information is available, whether due to missing components or incomplete information provided by a seller. This Master Dating Guide combines the Round Badge Era Guide with the Stop Sign Era Guide and adds a few years of the Square Badge Era of the 1980s to get to the Third Sequence of Serial Numbers.

Table 13
MASTER DATING GUIDE
GRETSCH DRUMS FROM ~1962 TO ~1984
© Richard E. Gier 2011, 2023
DO NOT COPY

Approx Year	Serial Approx Low	Number Approx High	Badge	Label	Model No.	Color	Lug Screw	Premium Strainer
1962	1001	6800	RB	OW1	Stamped	Black	R	Micro
1963	6800	18400	RB	OW1	Stamped	Black	R	Micro
1964	18400	35800	RB	OW1	Stamped	Black	R	Micro
1965	35800	55520	RB	OW1	Stamped	Black / Blue	R	Micro
1966	55520	78720	RB	OW1	Stamped	Black / Blue	R	Micro
1967	78720	97280	RB	OW1	Stamped	Black / Blue	R/H	Micro/L1
1968	97280	111200	RB	OW1	Stamped	Black / Blue	H	L1
1969	111200	122800	RB/SSB#1	OW1	Stamped	Black / Blue	H	L1
1970	122800	133800	SSB#1	OW1	Stamped	Black / Blue	H	L1
1971	133800	136500	SSB#1	OW1	Stamped	Black / Blue	H	L1
1971	00001	08300	SSB#1	OW1	Stamped	Black / Blue	H	L1
1972	08300	19300	SSB#1	OW1	Stamped	Black / Blue	H	L1
1973	19300	30300	SSB#1	OW1	Stamped/HW	Green/Black/Blue	H	L1/L2
1974	30300	41300	SSB#1	OW1	Handwritten	Green/Black/Blue	H	L2
1975	41300	52300	SSB#1	OW1/OW2	Handwritten	Green/Black/Blue	H	L2
1976	52300	63300	SSB#1	OW2	Handwritten	Green/Black/Blue	H	L2
1977	63300	74300	SSB#1/SQB#1	OW2*	Handwritten	Green/Black/Blue	H	L2
1978	74300	85300	SQB#1/SSB#2	OW2/OW3	Handwritten	Green/Black/Blue	H	L2
1979	85300	102300	SSB#2/SSB#3	OW3/GW1	Handwritten	Green/Black/Blue	H	L2
1980	102300	113300	SSB#3	GW1	Handwritten	Black / Blue	H	L2
1981	113300	125300	SSB#3	GW1	Handwritten	Black / Blue	H	L2
1982	125300	136300	SQB#2	GW1	Handwritten	Black / Blue	H	L2
1983	136300	147300	SQB#2	GW1/GW2	Handwritten	Black / Blue	H	L2
1984	147300	148500	SQB#2	GW2	Handwritten	Black / Blue	H	L2
1984	19780	higher	SQB#2	GW2	Handwritten	Black / Blue	H	L2

* Serial Numbers 66000 to 68000 had OW1 labels with blacked out guarantee language

Words of Caution. Assumptions involved with the Dating Guides above and detailed throughout this paper may not be totally accurate. They definitely do not produce precise, down-to-the-day date estimates,[88] so repeat after me:

‖: **THIS GUIDE CAN NOT BE TREATED AS FACT OR GOSPEL TRUTH!** :‖

---

[88] **DO NOT QUOTE OR CITE THIS GUIDE AS THE BASIS FOR A DEFINITIVE DATE OF A GRETSCH DRUM.** For those who want to use this guide when they list a drum for sale: Just provide all the relevant information and let the buyer determine the rest. There are too many misleading and misinformed sale listings already. Do not quote this paper or include a photo of this page as part of your listing. Serious Gretsch drum collectors will already have access to this paper and be able to estimate the age of a drum on their own.

Anyone who takes this guide and definitively declares the date of manufacture of a Gretsch drum is misusing the guide and is just simply not paying attention. This is one person's basis for the estimation of production years for Gretsch Round Badge and Stop Sign Badge drums. Variations will no doubt exist from the years predicted by this chart. This may not be enough to satisfy everyone's desire for precise manufacture dates for their vintage drums. However, no additional level of accuracy will be accomplished if points within the ranges are interpolated to provide greater precision. Conservatively, at best a one- or two- year range estimate seems achievable based upon the guide. However, the basic structure and rationale behind this guide should hold up even if some details are tweaked further with the benefit of additional data collection and analysis. Or, it may be partially superseded by Gretsch making its production records available. It should never be forgotten that the vintage drum world has many unexplained oddities. There will be drums which do not fit this guide. Some have been modified and are not original. Others simply do not fit. However, with this guide, the serial number becomes an additional tool that the one can use when evaluating a vintage Gretsch drum. The serial number should not be used in isolation, but should be considered along with numerous other physical characteristics when assessing a drum. Finally, despite all of the time and effort expended to create this guide, one should never forget that the way a drum sounds and looks is far more important than the date it was made.

Reports of drums which conform with or are exceptions to the date estimates provided by the guide are encouraged and welcome. If you can contribute information which would help to refine this analysis, please do. Every attempt has been made to include all reported drums in the analysis, even those which do not seem to fit, rather than simply ignoring the inconvenient truth of their existence. However, please be mindful that while exceptions will likely exist, this guide appears to work for the vast majority of Gretsch drums made during the 1960s and 1970s. Before you fire off an angry email describing your drum that does not fit this explanation, consider the bigger picture. You would not have read this far in the paper if this topic did not interest you. Help make future revisions better by reporting your drums and sharing what you know. That way the entire vintage drum community can benefit from your knowledge.

VII. SHERIDAN'S RULE REFINED

Sheridan's Rule serves as a helpful if not very precise guide for dating of Round Badge drums with serial numbers. When the Dating Guide is overlaid onto Sheridan's Rule, the estimates it provides can be improved. Sheridan's "early 60s" becomes the years 1962-1963 and involves 9,000 four-digit serial numbers. Sheridan's "mid-60s" becomes the years 1963-1968 and involves 90,000 five-digit serial numbers. The "late-60s" becomes the years 1968-1969 and involves 17,000 six-digit serial numbers. Based upon the additional research presented here, one should be very comfortable that lower five-digit serial numbers would be from the earlier part of the 1963-1968 range while higher ones would be from later in that period.[89]

---

[89] One individual with whom the author corresponded rejects Sheridan's Rule at least in part because a three piece set he bought in 1963 has five-digit serial numbers and therefore it is not from the "mid 60s" as Sheridan's Rule would estimate. The serial numbers are all in the 10XXX range, so they should fall just

Sheridan's Rule can be extended to address early Stop Sign Badge drums as well, as long as the serial numbers are from the First Sequence. Six-digit serial numbers are from the period 1969-1971. It should be emphasized that all of the serial numbers for the Round badge and early Stop Sign badge eras discussed here are from the First Sequence. When one encounters serial numbers from the Second and Third Sequences, Sheridan's Rule does not apply. This Dating Guide should provide reasonable estimates.

VIII. BADGE TIMELINE REFINED

A revised badge timeline can be extracted from the Master Dating Guide and compared to the timeline provided by Gretsch, and those presented in the Centennial and Badges Articles. Several differences are apparent. The SSB#1 appears earlier than previously understood. The SQB#1 makes its appearance before rather than after SSB#2. The large number of drums with SSB#3 badges reveals that the use of this badge was not as short as is generally thought. Future refinements to the revised timeline may be needed when additional reliable information becomes available.

Table 14
Badges Timeline Comparison
© Richard E. Gier 2011, 2023

Badge Style	Revised Timeline	Gretsch Provided	Centennial Article	Badges Article
Round	- 1969	1883 – 1971	– 1971	1930s – 1970
SSB#1	1969 - 1977	1972 – 1979	1971 -	1971 – roughly 1978
SQB#1	1977 – 1978	1980	1980 -	1980
SSB#2	1978 – 1979	1979 – 1980	Around 1979 -	1979 -
SSB#3	1979 – 1981	Early 1981	Early 1981 -	Late 1980 – late 1981
SQB#2	1982 -	1981 - Modern	Late 1981	Late 1981 -

IX. CONCLUSION

Gretsch serial numbers are useful tools in estimating a drum's manufacture date. They were applied in roughly numerical order starting in about 1962, with two restarts in number sequences, in about 1971 and again in about 1984. Sheridan's Rule is strongly supported by the patterns seen in data gathered from thousands of drums from the later Round badge and entire Stop Sign badge eras. Sheridan's Rule can be refined to provide closer date estimates for Round badge drums and extended to address dating of some Stop Sign badge drums. A Dating Guide is created to cover drums made for a more than two-decade span from about 1962 to about 1984. While no one can yet provide dates down the month and day, this guide is an improvement over previous resources.

---

after the "early 60s" and on the front end of the "mid-60s." Sheridan's Rule does not provide a precise estimate, just a rule of thumb. This Dating Guide suggests a 1963 date for these drums.

Acknowledgements:

Greg Webb started a thread on drumforum.org in 2006 and allowed me to join in on his project. Bill Maley was a frequent source of serial numbers, provided pictures and shared a healthy skepticism of the claims of many eBay sellers. Bill reviewed drafts and provided much valuable insight. John Sheridan authored the most detailed and informative articles on vintage Gretsch drums available when this guide was started in 2006. Rob Cook agreed to publish my original guide in 2011 while he was still working on The Gretsch Drum Book. Rob owns Rebeats and operates The Chicago Vintage and Custom Drum Show. Rob Cook, David Dudley, Bill Maley, Dave Michael, Kevin Oppendike, Steve Traversi, Pierre Van Craenenbroeck and Adam Willis provided pictures to illustrate different features of Gretsch drums. They retain rights in their pictures. Mike Bernazzani provided proofreading and editing help on this edition, but any errors are the author's. Many members of the online communities drumforum.org and vintagedrumforum.com and many eBay and Reverb sellers shared information.

About the Author:

A drummer through high school, Rick was out of the drum world for twenty years until buying a dirty three piece set at an auction. Only later did he discover the rarity of the all-original Gretsch Round Badge Progressive Jazz kit in Silver Glass Glitter. When not collecting and analyzing information on Gretsch drums, Rick assists entrepreneurs who are pursuing their dreams of small business ownership in the Kansas City area. His wonderful wife supports, or at least tolerates, his drum collecting and restoring efforts, despite the time and space that they consume.

Future Work:

Please contact the author with comments and reports of drums which can contribute to the understanding of Gretsch drums of this time period. His email address is: Rick@GretschDrumDatingguide.com. Feel free to report information using the form included on the next page. Updates to this paper and several other research projects involving vintage drums are available at www.GretschDrumDatingGuide.com.

Copyright Infringement:

The prior editions of this book suffered frequent infringement, so this note is added. The preparation of this book involved thousands of hours of hard work. The author retains all rights, including the right to reproduce, distribute, sell and display this work and to create derivative works based upon this work. You cannot scan or take a picture of an important table or graph and post it on an internet site - it violates the author's intellectual property rights. This is not excused by fair use exceptions to US Trademark law. It also does not matter that you did not make any money from this act – what matters is the impact on potential sales of the publication.

PLEASE HONOR THE AUTHOR'S CREATIVE RIGHTS.

Gretsch Serial Number Information Sheet

Serial Number: _____

Badge Style: RB   SSB#1   SQB#1   SSB#2   SSB#3   SQB#2

Label Style: OW1   OW2   OW3   GW1   GW2

Dimensions (inches):   Depth _____ x Diameter _____

Model Number: _____

Model Number: Stamped   Handwritten

Model Number Ink: Black   Blue   Green   Blank   Other _____

Model Number Size: Regular   Large

Model Number Font: Closed   Open

Lug Casing Attachment Screw: Round   Hexagonal   Slotted

Wrap or Finish: _____

Number of heads: One (Concert Tom)   Two

Throwoff Type: Microsensitive   Lightning #1   Lightning #2   Renown   Other_____

Set Configuration (depth x dia):   __x__, __x__, __x__, __x__, __x__, __x__, __x__

Model 4160 Snare Knurling: Yes   No

Purchase Date (if known): _____

Other information: _____

_____

_____

Email your reports to: Rick@GretschDrumDatingGuide.com

REBEATS PUBLICATIONS

THE GRETSCH DRUM BOOK by Rob Cook with John Sheridan Business history, dating guide

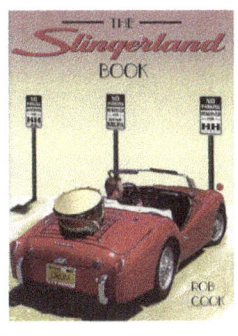
THE SLINGERLAND BOOK by Rob Cook Business history, dating guide

THE ROGERS BOOK by Rob Cook Business history, dating guide

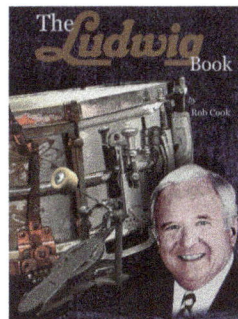
THE LUDWIG BOOK by Rob Cook Business history, dating guide

THE MAKING OF A DRUM COMPANY The autobiography of Wm. F. Ludwig II,

BEST SEAT IN THE HOUSE Jerry Shirley memoir

Franks For The Memories

LEEDY DRUM TOPICS

THE LEEDY WAY Biography of George Way, History of Leedy, Camco, Conn, L&S

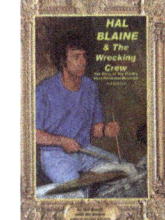
HAL BLAINE & THE WRECKING CREW Memoir of Hal Blaine, with Mr. Bonzai

Lucky Drummer Ed Shaughnessy memoir

GENE KRUPA, HIS LIFE AND TIMES biography of Gene Krupa,

Gretsch 1941 Catalog Reprint

THE BABY DODDS STORY

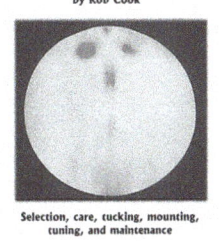
THE REBEATS CALFSKIN HEAD BOOK

George Way mini-bio, vendor directory

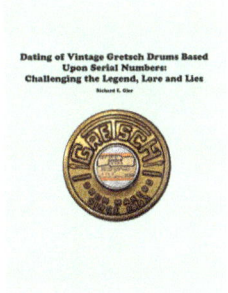
Gretsch Serial Number Dating Guide by Rick Gier

Ludwig Serial Number Dating Guide by Rick Gier

MY LIFE IN PERCUSSION Five Decades In The Music Products Industry Karl Dustman memoir

P.O. Box 6, Alma, Michigan 48801
989 463 4757
www.Rebeats.com   rob@rebeats.com

www.ingramcontent.com/pod-product-compliance
Lightning Source LLC
Chambersburg PA
CBHW051320110526
44590CB00031B/4419